THE COCKLESHELL RAID

Bordeaux 1942

KEN FORD

First published in 2010 by Osprey Publishing
Midland House, West Way, Botley, Oxford OX2 0PH, UK
44-02 23rd St, Suite 219, Long Island City, NY 11101, USA
E-mail: info@ospreypublishing.com

Print ISBN: 978 1 84603 693 4
PDF e-book ISBN: 978 1 84908 260 0

Page layout by: Bounford.com, Cambridge, UK
Index by Margaret Vaudrey
Typeset in Sabon
Maps by Bounford.com, Cambridge, UK
3D BEVs by Paul Kime
Originated by PPS Grasmere Ltd, Leeds, UK
Printed in China through Worldprint Ltd

10 11 12 13 14   10 9 8 7 6 5 4 3 2 1

A CIP catalog record for this book is available from the British Library

THE WOODLAND TRUST

Osprey Publishing are supporting the Woodland Trust, the UK's leading woodland conservation charity, by funding the dedication of trees.

FOR A CATALOGUE OF ALL BOOKS PUBLISHED BY OSPREY MILITARY AND AVIATION PLEASE CONTACT:

Osprey Direct, c/o Random House Distribution Center, 400 Hahn Road, Westminster, MD 21157
Email: uscustomerservice@ospreypublishing.com

Osprey Direct, The Book Service Ltd, Distribution Centre, Colchester Road, Frating Green, Colchester, Essex, CO7 7DW
E-mail: customerservice@ospreypublishing.com

www.ospreypublishing.com

IMPERIAL WAR MUSEUM COLLECTIONS

Many of the photos in this book come from the Imperial War Museum's huge collections which cover all aspects of conflict involving Britain and the Commonwealth since the start of the twentieth century. These rich resources are available online to search, browse and buy. In addition to Collections Online, you can visit the Visitor Rooms where you can explore over 8 million photographs, thousands of hours of moving images, the largest sound archive of its kind in the world, thousands of diaries and letters written by people in wartime, and a huge reference library. To make an appointment, call (020) 7416 5320, or e-mail mail@iwm.org.uk. Imperial War Museum www.iwm.org.uk

ARTIST'S NOTE

Readers may care to note that the original paintings from which the colour battlescene plates in this book were prepared are available for private sale. All reproduction copyright whatsoever is retained by the Publishers. All enquiries should be addressed to:

Howard Gerrard
11 Oaks Road
Tenterden
Kent
TN30 6RD
UK

The Publishers regret that they can enter into no correspondence upon this matter.

AUTHOR'S NOTE

Boom Patrol Boat (BPB)
Chief of Combined Operations (CCO)
Combined Operations (CO)
Combined Operations Development Centre (CODC)
Combined Operations Pilotage Parties (COPPs)
Distinguished Service Medal (DSM)
Distinguished Service Order (DSO)
Judge Advocate General (JAG)
Non-Commissioned Officer (NCO)
Royal Air Force (RAF)
Royal Marine Boom Patrol Detachment (RMBPD)
Saunders Rowe (SARO)
Sea Reconnaissance Unit (SRU)
Second Major Naval Base Defence Organisation (MNBDO II)
Sicherheitsdienst (SD)

EDITOR'S NOTE

For ease of comparison between types, Imperial/American measurements are used almost exclusively throughout this book. The following data will help in converting the Imperial/American measurements to metric:

1 mile = 1.6km

1lb = 0.45kg

1yd = 0.9m

1ft = 0.3m

1in. = 2.54cm/25.4mm

1gal = 4.5 liters

1 ton (US) = 0.9 tonnes

ACKNOWLEDGEMENTS

I should like to express my gratitude to the Trustees of the Imperial War Museum, the Royal Marines Museum and the Combined Services Museum of Maldon, Essex for permission to use the photographs for which they hold the copyright. Personal thanks also go to John Ambler and Matthew Little of the Royal Marines Museum, Marilyn Bullivant and Richard Wooldridge of the Combined Services Museum and to Carol Blasco in Bordeaux for their help during the preparation of this book.

CONTENTS

INTRODUCTION

During 1942 the war between Britain and Germany was not confined just to the battlefields of Europe and North Africa, for both sides were also engaged in the routine operations associated with economic warfare. The two countries were each attempting to undermine the manufacturing capability of their enemy by trying to choke off the other's supply lines, since both relied on imported raw materials to maintain their war efforts. Neither side had easy access to all its needs and had to resort to shipping supplies across hostile seas.

Germany was more fortunate in that it gained most of its resources from within the territories it had overrun and captured. Britain relied to a much greater extent on shipping imports from around the world and the Nazi regime went to great lengths to interfere with these supplies through a vigorous campaign of U-boat attacks. In reply Britain attempted to place a blockage across the sea routes used by the Axis powers. Unfortunately, the task of trying to police the sea lanes of the world looking for individual enemy ships was almost impossible. A few German vessels, popularly known as 'blockade busters' or 'blockade runners', managed to slip through the cordon and evade the Royal Navy's and Royal Air Force's best efforts to sink them.

During 1942 the Ministry of Economic Warfare began to evaluate the importance of these ships to the enemy. It concluded that the vessels trading with Japan and the Far East were carrying freight that had a strategic value far above the simple tonnage that they carried, for their cargoes were not bulk shipments of war materials but consignments of special and highly prized items such as rubber, tin, manganese tunstate (tungsten) and specific animal oils. All of these products were vital to German and Italian manufacturing processes. The blockade runners, however, were just one of the many problems facing the nation at that time. This period, the third year of the war, was not a particularly good one for the British. It was true that the USA had entered the conflict in December 1941 and given the nation hope that the progress of the war was at last going to improve, but it would take time for America's contribution to become effective. In the meantime it was down to Britain and her Commonwealth to contain the Axis powers in Europe and North Africa, while Stalin's forces tried to deal with the German invasion of the Soviet Union. In none of these theatres was the war going well for the Allies: Hitler's attack on Russia was driving its way inexorably towards Moscow and deep into the USSR's satellite states; Rommel's Gazala offensive in North Africa was pushing the British back into Egypt and the all-conquering Japanese onslaught in the Far East was showing no sign of faltering. At the sea the U-boat war looked as though it was being won by the enemy.

The air analysis of the RAF's bombing offensive against Germany was showing signs that it was becoming costly and mostly ineffective.

Across the Channel France was a divided nation, occupied in the north by Germany and in the south by the Vichy regime under Marshal Pétain. The administration at Vichy was no more than a puppet government intent on trying to please, or at least trying not to aggravate, its Nazi masters. Its police and militia operated under German instructions and were compliant with all orders issued to them by the occupying powers in the north, including rounding up Jews and other foreign nationals, and seeking out and handing over all enemies of the Third Reich, which of course included any British servicemen found in the country.

At home, the nation's morale was lifted to some extent by the exploits of Britain's Combined Operations (CO) organization. Significant raids against German forces in occupied territories organized by CO had grabbed the headlines. Successful operations at Vaagso and Lofoten in 1941 and the spectacular assault against the dry dock in St Nazaire in March 1942[1], both made by commandos ably assisted by the Royal Navy, demonstrated to the public that the country's fighting spirit was alive and well. The mood was tempered somewhat by the disaster that befell the Canadians when they launched a large-scale raid on Dieppe in August 1942[2]. The attempted landings were a disaster and over half of the 6,000 men who took part were killed. Nonetheless, the appetite for specialist operations that reaped high rewards survived but it remained to be seen whether such a raid could be planned to tackle the problem of the 'blockade busters'.

During the early part of the war Combined Operations raids against enemy occupied targets were no more that small night-time attacks with limited success. In December 1941 this changed when a large party of commandos was landed at Vaagso in Norway and took control of the whole town during daylight hours wreaking great destruction to German installations. (IWM N459)

1 See Campaign 92: *St Nazaire 1942* by Ken Ford (Osprey Publishing)
2 See Campaign 127: *Dieppe 1942* by Ken Ford (Osprey Publishing)

ORIGINS OF THE RAID

The concerns felt by the Ministry of Economic Warfare about the blockade busters were given a higher profile when on 9 May 1942 its minister, Lord Selborne, raised the matter with the Prime Minister, Winston Churchill. He asked for something to be done to stop or interfere with the trade between Germany and the Far East. Since the Nazi invasion of Russia in June 1941, the Trans-Siberian rail route to the Far East had been closed to Axis traffic and resulted in the continuation of trade between Germany and Japan becoming entirely dependent on seaborne means.

There was a limited number of ships under German control capable of making voyages from Europe to the Far East, either by Cape Horn or the Cape of Good Hope, without bunkering en route. If this relatively small number could be reduced further, then the trade would be seriously affected. Some of the vessels were commandeered French ships of the Vichy regime, but most were German. By mid-1942 the total number of these ships was believed not to exceed 26. Fifteen potential blockade runners were at that time awaiting cargoes in French Atlantic ports and they were expected to sail before the end of the month.

Lord Selborne explained the scale and importance of the trade and cited that in the 12 voyages completed between July 1941 and May 1942, approximately 25,000 tons of crude rubber had passed through the port of Bordeaux to Germany and Italy and during that period six or seven ships had left the port for the Far East. He estimated that if the traffic was maintained at that level, Germany's war requirements of crude rubber would be met and that there would be considerable spare tonnage space for other valuable cargoes. He also noted that the traffic was two-way, as Japan required specialized equipment for manufacturing processes, prototypes of various weapons and other special component parts for arms and equipment. Germany was, he went on, trying to meet those needs with the tonnage space available in the blockade busters. Even just a few of these cargoes would appreciably strengthen both Germany's and Japan's war efforts.

The matter of interdicting this trade was referred by the Prime Minister to the Chiefs of Staff Committee for it to consider a military solution to the problem. Such a resolution was not easy to find, for the blockade runners were just a few single ships that easily became lost to the British in the huge wastes of the Atlantic and Indian Oceans and in the desolate seas around the capes.

The quayside at Bordeaux, now turned into a public promenade. The German blockade busters attacked by Maj Hasler and Cpl Sparks in the raid were tied up along this section of the River Garonne. (Ken Ford)

The main base for these enemy ships was Bordeaux in France, an inland port some 60 miles from the Atlantic coast up the Gironde and Garonne rivers. It was a perfect harbour from which to operate the blockade runners. Bordeaux was sufficiently far from the open water to render itself safe from naval bombardment, it had immediate access to the Atlantic Ocean, and its quays and facilities were strung out along the banks of the wide River Garonne. This meant that it was an almost impossible target to strike from the air. The only material thing the Chiefs of Staff Committee could do was to refer the problem to the three services – the Royal Navy, the Royal Air Force (RAF) and the army – and to the Combined Operations HQ for further consideration.

All three services reviewed the options available to them to meet the Chiefs of Staff's directive. With the ships sailing singly and at irregular intervals it would be costly, time consuming and hazardous for the Royal Navy to attempt to blockade the port. The navy also decided that there was little it could do once the ships had entered the river on their way up to the inland harbour. Seemingly the navy could only continue its efforts to intercept the vessels while they were at sea, with mixed results.

The RAF considered how it might affect the trade by aerial bombardment. Precision raids at this time, however, were quite inaccurate and the chances of hitting individual vessels moored alongside long quays were minimal. Massed bombing against the whole of the port facilities would cause great material damage and loss of life to French civilians, as the harbour was situated right in the centre of the city. The Foreign Office was against the bombing of any French target that might incur appreciable numbers of civilian deaths. It claimed that such raids would adversely affect public opinion in France and amongst the Free French forces fighting with Britain in North Africa and the Middle East. The RAF concluded that its main involvement, like the navy's, would be to attempt to intercept the vessels at sea. It did also volunteer to continue laying mines at the mouth of the Gironde.

The army contemplated an attack by land against Bordeaux; in effect an invasion from the sea and an advance in a direct line of over 30 miles to attack the city. Such an operation would most likely involve three divisions, huge numbers of landing craft and massive air and naval support. Clearly such an attack would be very difficult to mount at that time and would inevitably be a very precarious enterprise. The lessons of the Dieppe raid showed that Britain still had a lot to learn about launching punitive amphibious raids against the fortified coast of France. That left Combined Operations as they only other group who might be able to tackle the problem.

Combined Operations HQ, with the limited resources available to it, was also at a loss to know how to tackle the problem of the blockade busters. A raid to attack and sink the ships would require a large amount of explosives to be placed by hand in key positions on the vessels. If the raid was mounted from the sea the commando force would have to carry these demolition charges, weapons and other vital stores approximately 60 miles upstream to Bordeaux, past coastal defences and enemy positions, through areas patrolled by French police and their informers, right into the centre of the city to the wharves lining the river front. Not an easy or viable task. Landing a raiding force by parachute would face the same problems getting to the ships. It was likely that neither of these methods would gain their objectives, and if the attackers did manage to plant and blow their explosives, few of the troops taking part would be able to successfully make their way back to the rescue ships waiting offshore, through a countryside alerted to their presence.

Up until that time raids planned by Combined Operations HQ had been tip-and-run affairs along the coast. Raiding parties either landed and were evacuated by sea, such as in the Lofoten and Vaagso raids in Norway as well as the Dieppe raid in France, or landed by parachute and withdrawn by sea as in the raid on the Bruneval radar station in northern France during Operation *Biting* in 1942. Bordeaux was too far inland for the adoption of either of these tactics and was also well guarded by the enemy.

After their invasion of 1940 the Germans had taken steps to defend Bordeaux and the Atlantic coast nearby. The city was a valuable harbour to the enemy but was also the home of a U-boat flotilla, and massive concrete submarine pens were under construction in its inner basin. The depth of these defences in 1942 was nowhere near the level that would be built later in the war, when the likelihood of an Allied invasion became more of a possibility, but they were still formidable. These installations were ringed with flak batteries manned by Luftwaffe anti-aircraft personnel. Further flak positions guarded the estuary of the Gironde, along with a number of large-calibre coast defence batteries and radar stations. Garrisoning the whole area around Bordeaux was the 708th Infantry Division.

The response from Combined Operations HQ during the summer of 1942 to the request from the Chiefs of Staff was that it would continue looking into the subject of the blockade busters, but, like the other services, it could offer no immediate solution to the problem. Lord Louis Mountbatten, Head of Combined Operations, left the matter with his planners on the Search and Examination Committees.

At the time of the raid on Bordeaux, Lord Louis Mountbatten was the head of Combined Operations. Churchill chose him to replace the aging Admiral Roger Keyes. The move caused great surprise within military circles for Mountbatten was a relatively junior officer with the lowly rank of captain. The fact that he was a cousin to the King no doubt helped Churchill make the appointment. Mountbatten was quickly elevated to rear-admiral in order to take a seat on the Chiefs of Staff Committee and later proved himself to be a resourceful and energetic commander of Special Forces. (IWM TR1230)

INITIAL STRATEGY

Although Combined Operations could offer no immediate solution to the problem of the German blockade busters, the organization did have a team located at Portsmouth that was working on exploring methods of attacking ships in harbour. A very small group called the Combined Operations Development Centre (CODC) was devising new ways and methods of striking back at the enemy. Part of the group, under the command of a Royal Marine officer, Maj H. G. 'Blondie' Hasler, was specifically looking at various means of attacking ships with small parties of men. In 1941 Hasler had proposed that such raids could be mounted by canoe or by underwater swimmers. His ideas were rejected as being unworkable – canoes were too fragile for major tasks and underwater swimming was in its infancy. A little later the success of Italian frogmen, together with their development of exploding motor boats and two-man 'human torpedoes', led to a rethink.

The methods the Italians employed in their motor boats were fairly crude. The craft was intended to enter harbour at high speed and be aimed at a particular vessel. Once locked on to its target the pilot would eject out of the back of the craft while the boat, packed with a large explosive charge, continued to its objective. The vessel would then explode on impact. The unfortunate pilot, stuck in the water with no means of escape, surrendered to the enemy. Of course, such an attack would first have to negotiate the boom defences that barred entry into most harbours, so the location of the target vessels under attack was particularly important.

As part of his investigation into attacking enemy ships in harbour by covert means, Hasler was asked early in 1942 to develop a British version of the exploding motor boat. The craft was given the codename 'Boom Patrol Boat' (BPB). He was also ordered to look into ways of improving the performance of underwater swimmers. Combined Operations planners especially liked the idea of the exploding boat and Hasler immediately began working with Vosper Shipbuilders on the construction of a suitable craft. One thing bothered those involved and that was the matter of the boat's single crewman being forced to surrender to the enemy. Such an action went against the accepted British manner of waging war. It was each serviceman's duty and, indeed, personal intent to evade capture by the enemy at every opportunity. A method had to be devised that would give the pilot of the BPB at least a chance of escaping.

Maj Hasler had spent his life enjoying the pleasures of small craft and had been sailing in the sheltered waters of Langstone Harbour close to Portsmouth since he was a boy. He was very much at home on the water, fascinated by all types of small boats, and was intrigued by the agility and flexibility of canoes. He knew that the craft was light and vulnerable in rough water, but he also appreciated that they were silent and manoeuvrable enough to penetrate enemy defences at night unseen. To his mind they could be the perfect vessels from which to attack ships inside enemy harbours.

During his time with CODC Hasler continued to work with canoes. In the early part of 1942 two ranks from No. 6 Commando were attached to him for experimental work. With the agreement of the Commander-in-Chief Portsmouth, Hasler and his small party carried out night exercises in conjunction with the operational patrol that guarded the Eastern Boom across the Solent, protecting the approaches to the naval base. New techniques were developed for counter-attacking human torpedoes and other enemy craft with specially equipped canoes. His work made him realize that the standard canoe then in use by the navy, the Cockle Mk I, was not as effective as it might be.

This interest in the canoe and the problems associated with the use of Boom Patrol Boats set Hasler thinking. If the two types of craft were deployed together, the crew of the canoes could help the BPBs negotiate enemy boom defences and then act as a means of escape for their pilots. He felt sure that this proposition could be the solution to overcome the constraints associated with the BPBs. Hasler spoke to his senior officer at the Combined Operations Development Centre, Capt T. A. Hussey, about his idea. Hussey received the details regarding the use of canoes with the BPBs with some enthusiasm. The two men realized that the crews of these two types of craft would have to train together and be conversant with each other's tasks to be effective. It soon became obvious that a specialized unit would have to be formed and trained to operate the vessels, clearly a task for the Royal Marines.

Hasler was given permission to speak to the planners at the Combined Operations HQ in Richmond Terrace in London to discuss the possibility of raising a specific boom patrol boat unit. To add strength to his case, he also suggested that the unit could act in concert with the Royal Navy, helping to secure the effectiveness of the defence booms already in position guarding Portsmouth Harbour. There was some initial resistance to the raising of yet another specialized unit, but the interest already being shown in the idea of explosive motor boats ensured that the proposal would be seriously considered at the highest level of COHQ nonetheless.

On 12 May 1942 the commandant of CODC, LtCol H. Langley, presented a proposal to the Chief of Combined Operations (CCO), Lord Louis Mountbatten, for the formation of the Royal Marine Harbour Patrol Detachment. Langley explained that the main disadvantage with the BPB was the difficulty it would have negotiating boom defences, for the craft's design made it doubtful whether it could pass over any form of surface obstruction in darkness without some assistance. He proposed to overcome this difficulty with canoes ('cockles' as they were known in the navy) that would be developed to work in conjunction with the BPBs. The BPBs would approach the objective together with the cockles who would then perform the following functions:

(a) clear a passage through the surface obstructions using explosive cutters or, preferably, some as yet undetermined silent method
(b) take station by the gap and exhibit some form of screened leading light until the BPBs had passed through
(c) follow up the BPBs for the remainder of their approach with the object of picking up their drivers once they had 'baled out'.

Two commandos attempt to secure a Bren gun in the bows of a flimsy Folbot as it is rocked by the swirling surf. This type of collapsible canoe was the forerunner of the more sturdy cockles later used by the RMBPD. (Royal Marines Museum Collection)

Smoke flares could also be used at this stage to give some concealment. In order to achieve the close liaison necessary, Langley explained, it was evident that the crews of both the BPBs and the cockles should be trained as a single unit, with its men interchangeable between the two tasks. The crews of both craft could also operate completely independently if required. The entire unit would be under the control of CO, since its main function was bound up with combined operations and raiding.

Langley made it clear that the unit should comprise entirely of Royal Marines. He gave several reasons for this point of view, explaining that the execution of such an attack is a typical

Royal Marine role, calling for close cooperation with the Royal Navy. Its participants would need ability in commando-type fighting and they would have to have a good deal of 'sea sense'. The success of the operation would rest entirely on the individual morale of the men concerned and it was felt that this could be best achieved by starting with a strong foundation of *esprit de corps* such as that found in the Royal Marines. In addition, all officers and men in the unit would be carefully selected from volunteers. Langley, with Maj Hasler's support, had put together a soundly argued and compelling proposal.

On 20 May, Mountbatten agreed and approved the proposition. He gave the go-ahead for the unit to be formed under the title The Royal Marine Boom Patrol Detachment (RMBPD), with Maj Hasler as the officer commanding. The authorized detachment would consist of a commanding officer of major rank, a second-in-command with the rank of captain, and two sections each with a lieutenant, a sergeant, two corporals and ten marines. In addition, there would be a four-man Administration Section (sergeant, orderly, storeman and driver) and a Maintenance Section made up of attached naval personnel. This gave a total Royal Marine complement of 34 men.

Soon afterwards a circular was issued and sent around various Royal Marine units calling for volunteers for hazardous duties. It explained that the work would consist of offensive operations of a 'commando' type, calling for exceptional individual qualities. The virtues required by all officers and men were clearly laid out in the circular: each man needed to be eager to engage the enemy, indifferent to his own personal safety, intelligent, nimble, free from strong family ties or dependants, able to swim and of good physique with excellent eyesight. It was not essential to have any previous knowledge of the sea or small boats, although such knowledge would be an advantage.

The process of interviewing likely candidates for the unit soon began. Hasler had already found a suitable contender as his second-in-command, Capt J. D. 'Jock' Stewart, who had served with him in the Royal Marines Fortress Unit in Norway. Stewart was then serving with the Second Major Naval Base Defence Organisation (MNBDO II) a formation held in readiness to organize the defence of any captured naval harbours abroad and was eager to join a unit that looked like it would soon see action. Hasler's two chosen section commanders, Lt J. W Mackinnon and Lt W. A. Pritchard-Gordon, were enthusiastic young officers not long out of training. The bulk of the RMBPD were recruited from volunteers of the Plymouth Division. Hasler selected two sergeants, three corporals and 28 marines as being suitable. They were formed into a squad and put through a course of parade training, swimming, PE and initiative exercises. During this period a few dropped out and some replacements were added to the original group. At the end of the course 23 marines were finally selected to join the unit. This number was three in excess of establishment, but it was proposed to weed out the surplus during future training. On 23 July they moved to their new headquarters in Southsea.

Hasler's RMBPD was located in two Nissen huts alongside the old Victorian Lumps Fort. The site was on the promenade of the seaside resort, just yards from the beach right opposite the Eastern Boom, which stretched across the Solent from the fort to Seaview on the Isle of Wight. Throughout its six-mile, dog-legged course the boom's posts and underwater obstacles restricted seagoing traffic entering the Solent. A few hundred yards to the east was the Royal Marine Barracks at Eastney. Two miles to the west, the Royal Navy's major dockyard at Portsmouth dominated the scene.

The men were billeted in nearby private residences. They had been given the same privileges as commandos and would receive the six shillings and eight pence per day for their accommodation and subsistence. Such an arrangement gave the men a degree of

OPERATION *FRANKTON* OFFICERS

Maj H. G. 'Blondie' Hasler

Herbert George 'Blondie' Hasler was born in Dublin on 27 February 1914. His father was a Warrant Officer in the Royal Army Medical Corps who was drowned when his ship was torpedoed en route to Salonika in 1917. From an early age Hasler became involved in working with small craft, sailing boats and canoes and these craft remained his main interest for the rest of his life. Blondie Hasler was commissioned into the Royal Marines in 1932. His early military career saw him serve with the Mobile Naval Base Unit in Egypt in 1935/36. He was promoted to captain just before war broke out and served as Fleet Landing Officer at Scapa Flow. He later took part in Anglo/French operations at Narvik in Norway where he was awarded the OBE and the Croix de Guerre as well as being Mentioned in Dispatches. After Operation *Frankton* he continued with the development of small craft for military purposes. Post-war he achieved great recognition for his work in the field of yachting, most notably for his development work in self-steeringgear. He died in 1987.

Lt J. W. Mackinnon

Jack Mackinnon was born in Oban in Argyllshire on 15 July 1921 and later lived in Glasgow with his parents. He joined the Royal Marines after working in an office before the war. He served in the ranks for almost two years before earning his commission in early 1942. Mackinnon passed out of officer training school almost at the top of his intake and was quickly brought to the notice of Blondie Hasler when he was looking for fit young officers to join his new unit. Operation *Frankton* was to be Mackinnon's first action.

independence, but also required them to show great responsibility. They were expected to be self-reliant and not to abuse the privilege of being free from service life when off duty. They were given this commando allowance in recognition of the fact that their training and work would consist of many night exercises, with unconventional hours for eating and sleeping. As their training progressed it would also be necessary for them to frequently change their locations. Another major factor was that the small unit had no personnel for non-operational administrative duties – no cooks, guards or anyone to do fatigues. The officers would likewise live away from normal messes and barracks, located in a private apartment overlooking Southsea Boating Lake.

Prior to the arrival of the main body, one sergeant, two corporals and three marines, previously selected at Plymouth by Hasler, moved to Southsea to become qualified trainers. Maj Hasler had discovered that there were no instructors available for small

Dolphin Court, overlooking the boating lake at Southsea. Maj Hasler and his officers of the RMBPD were housed in the first-floor apartment on the extreme right of the building. The boating lake had itself some small claim to fame during the early part of the war, for initial development work to deal with the then new threat of German magnetic mines was carried out on the lake in rowing boats by men from the mine warfare section of HMS *Vernon*. (Ken Ford)

boat work other than him, so he began the task of training these men to become trainers. For three weeks he put the marines and his officers through a stiff programme of sea training as well as learning how to handle canoes, assault boats, RAF dinghies and many other craft, in all weathers, during daylight hours as well as at night.

When the bulk of his unit arrived Hasler still continued to be fully engaged in helping the men and the instructors obtain proficiency in seamanship, small-arms fire, handling explosives, swimming (including breaststroke, freestyle, surface diving and lifesaving) as well as general physical training. The major was insistent that the men obtain improved muscle development, particularly in the arms. Good physical condition was paramount; the unit was on course to be the fittest in the whole corps.

Hasler's system was to demonstrate the correct method in all things, then allow the class to carry out his lesson before commentating on their performance. He dictated notes on all aspects of this training, which were subsequently used as instructors' handbooks, as much of what was being taught lay outside that contained in the normal navy and army textbooks. In time Hasler handed all of his training work over to his officers and the instructors so that he could concentrate on his role as commander. Each week all ranks were given a personal report pointing out their strengths and weaknesses. Throughout this specialized training it was never forgotten that all of them belonged to the Royal Marines. The regular non-commissioned officers (NCOs) ensured that parade-ground behaviour and the long-established demeanour of the corps were maintained throughout.

The RMBPD had primarily been raised to train on the explosive motor boat and to develop methods of using this type of craft to attack enemy ships. The development of a British-designed craft was underway with Vosper Shipbuilders, and Hasler continued to monitor its progress at the same time as he was schooling his fledgling unit in the black arts of clandestine operations. Various ideas for deploying the BPB were considered, including the possibility of dropping it from an aircraft close to its target. Such development work took a considerable amount of time to evolve and it became clear that the new weapon would not be available to be used operationally for a long while. In the meantime Hasler continued with his idea of using canoes in an offensive role. Indeed, much of the training undertaken by the unit revolved around the use of these cockles.

The Cockle Mk I originally used by the RMBPD had several limitations as it was somewhat fragile and prone to develop leaks. Hasler was fully aware of these faults and had been working on a replacement for some time. The major felt that covert operations in enemy territory needed a craft of more robust construction with certain

The ground beside the old Victorian coast defences of Lumps Fort at Southsea. In this area the RMBPD was housed in Nissen huts just a few yards from the beach. The base was right opposite the Eastern Boom defences that guarded the anchorage of the Solent and the entrance to the Royal Navy's premier dockyard at Portsmouth. The remains of this boom can still be seen today marching out across the Solent to the Isle of Wight. (Ken Ford)

MAY 20 1942

Royal Marine Boom Patrol Detachment is formed.

Maj Hasler and Capt Stewart use single paddles to 'walk' a Cockle Mk II down the beach and into the water. This method of launching the canoe demonstrates the sturdy construction of the craft and the success of the wooden runners along its keel, which enable the cockle to be manhandled across rough ground. (Royal Marines Museum Collection)

features added for this particular function. Across the Solent at Cowes on the Isle of Wight the aircraft manufacturer Saunders Rowe (SARO) had experience in fabric and plywood design in their SARO Laminated Woods subsidiary. It was to this company, and in particular their works manager Fred Goatley, that Maj Hasler turned regarding the building of a new type of cockle.

Hasler needed a strong two-man canoe with a rigid bottom that could be dragged across rough ground such as a shingle beach without tearing out its underside. It had to be capable of carrying a 150lb load, handling rough water and staying afloat when swamped. As it was likely to need transporting to its operational area by stealth, its beam or width had to be sufficiently narrow to allow it to pass through the forward torpedo hatch of a submarine. The craft would also need to lie low in the water with a slender silhouette.

While Hasler and his team trained together and bonded into an efficient unit, the problem of the German blockade runners was still causing great concern within the corridors of the Ministry of Economic Warfare. The Minister, Lord Selborne, wrote to the Prime Minister's Office on 9 May, followed up by another letter on 22 June, pleading for something to be done regarding the enemy seaborne traffic. Six weeks later, on 5 August, an even more urgent minute was dispatched to the Prime Minister. Lord Selborne was gravely concerned with the scale of traffic between Germany and Japan and the effect their exchange of goods and services was having upon the war potential of the two Axis powers. 'Hardly a day passes,' wrote the minister, 'without my seeing convincing proof of the determination of both countries to execute their programme. Now Italy, too, is planning to resuscitate her starved war industries with raw materials from the Far East. The importance of this traffic is no less today than when I wrote my previous minutes. If immediate action could be taken it should not be too late.' Once again the problem was passed over to the Chiefs of Staff Committee, and once again the difficulties in dealing with the dilemma were considered by the various services, before being put aside yet again. The problem also settled on the desks of the planners at Combined Operations. The mission had already been given the title Operation *Frankton*, but no clear method had been devised as to how it could be solved. In the planning department, LtCol Horton continued to ponder long and hard as to how the enemy blockade runners could be eliminated by the light forces of Combined Operations.

PLANNING AND TRAINING

In addition to the training already discussed, the War Diary of RMBPD shows that they also received instruction in navigation, including tides and winds, and their effect on small craft, chart reading, the use of a compass as well as an understanding of compass deviations and magnetic variations. This training was first put into practice on 10 August, when No. 1 Section attempted to reach the Isle of Wight in canoes during rough weather. The attempt failed, as high winds and rough seas swamped the three boats. The crews managed to climb out of their craft and swim to the boom to await rescue, and a passing boat from HMS *Dolphin* patrol later picked them up. Fortunately all three canoes were salvaged later that day. The experience showed that the group still had much to learn, and training continued daily to hone the skills required for clandestine offensive action.

Two months into the life of the unit the Cockle Mk II was available in prototype form and put through a tough testing regime. By then all the men had been trained in various techniques associated with stealth operations and were at a peak of physical fitness. The RMBPD had become an elite unit, full of confidence in its own abilities. There was still no sign of the explosive motor boats being ready for deployment, so work continued on sharpening their operational skills in other small craft, most notably canoes. At this stage there was still some way to go before all men were up to speed on navigation and seamanship, but they were gradually perfecting all the other attributes of a close-knit fighting team.

On 18 September Maj Hasler was passing through London and had the chance to drop into COHQ in Richmond Terrace. He met with Col Robert Neville, the Chief Planning Coordinator. Hasler informed Neville that his team was making such good progress that they were almost ready to undertake an operation. Neville was reportedly surprised that the unit was ready after such a short time and, although it was probably premature at this stage, allowed Hasler to view a few files outlining possible raids then under consideration. Hasler studied the proposals but did not consider any of them suitable for the particular skills of his unit.

A few days later Col Neville informed his senior planner, LtCol Horton, about Hasler's visit and the work he was doing on creating a team suitable for small craft operations. Horton realized that perhaps Hasler's team could provide the solution to

Two crewmen from the RMBPD exercising in a Cockle Mk II off Lumps Fort at Southsea. One of the Nissen huts that formed the unit's base and the steps leading to the beach can be seen in the mid-background. (Royal Marines Museum Collection)

the blockade busters. On 21 September Hasler returned to COHQ to be given the news that there was an operation under consideration that might interest him. Hasler was given the file on Operation *Frankton* and asked to try to put together a workable plan to undertake the mission.

Maj Hasler was immediately attracted by the scheme. He realized at once that his canoes could approach the ships unseen if they could get in close enough to attack. He spent the day studying the problems associated with travelling up the river to Bordeaux, the tides, the moon phases and the enemy opposition. By the end of the day he had arrived at the makings of a practical solution: the cockles could be transported to the mouth of the river by submarine at night, then paddled the 60 miles upriver in stages – moving by night and lying up by day – ready to attack the enemy ships in Bordeaux with limpet mines under the cover of darkness. Escape could be arranged by moving back downriver, if possible, or overland if not, to a rendezvous point with a submarine a few days later.

That evening he discussed his scheme with Col Neville. The Chief Planning Coordinator agreed with the basic outline plan that Hasler had sketched out. If successful, such a mission could be the solution to a problem that had been causing disquiet to the government at the highest level for some time. Hasler was now asked to formulate a detailed operational plan for *Frankton* with the planners at Combined Operations, which could be put before a meeting of the whole COHQ and the Combined Chiefs of Staff Committee for approval.

Hasler returned to Southsea in a state of high excitement. His unit now had a purpose and a definite objective towards which their training could be focused. For security reasons the method of the attack and its objective had to be kept secret from the whole of the team during the preparation stages. There would have to be a sharp ramping-up of development and familiarization work on the new Cockle Mk II, but there now seemed, at last, to be a specific goal in sight and a clear objective to work towards.

Steps leading to the beach from the esplanade at Southsea close by the RMBPD base. Lumps Fort can be clearly seen in the background. The beach has been raised since the war with the deposit of large amounts of shingle; in 1942 the wall was 4ft higher than today. To maintain fitness and initiative, Maj Hasler forbade the use of these steps, so boats, cockles and equipment all had to be manhandled up and down the 8ft-high wall like an obstacle course. (Ken Ford)

Hasler's outline plan now had to be converted into a detailed operational scheme, capable of convincing those in authority that it was worth the risk and had a high chance of success. To ease his burden, Hasler took his second-in-command, Capt Stewart, into his confidence and the two of them set about gathering all the background information required for the plan from a variety of sources. While the two officers concentrated on the project the rest of the unit undertook a new range of tasks specifically geared to the raid.

The War Diary for the RMBPD shows the changes in the type of activities undertaken after Hasler's 21 September meeting with the CO planners. On the 27th of the month normal working hours were rearranged to allow for more night training. Both No. 1 and No. 2 Sections worked from 0830–1330 hours, then each section would work alternate nights from 1900–0500 hours. Most days included canoe work, especially during rough weather conditions, as familiarization with boat handling in heavy seas was crucial. On 9 and 10 October the diary shows that the sections practised both silent approaches and stalking sentries, along with the stripping and assembling of weapons in the dark. Two days later they were weightlifting at sea from canoes! On 17 October Hasler lectured on dockyards, and further compass training was also given to the unit. By 24 October more specific training for the operation was also initiated, with the marines erecting iron plating to represent the sides of a ship and practising placing limpet mines. On 30 October, No. 1 Section, the group Hasler had selected for the operation, went north to Scotland to join the submarine depot ship HMS *Forth* to continue the training specific to Operation *Frankton*. As a cover to protect the secrecy of the planned operation, however, the move was described as being for practice in advanced training techniques.

In the meantime Hasler and Stewart worked on finalizing their plan, as well as working with SARO on the finer details of the Cockle Mk II, which was so essential to the operation. Prototypes were available to the unit, but some further modifications were still required. The final design was a 16ft-long craft with a beam of 28 inches. Its depth, when erected and in use, was 11 inches, but the cockle could be collapsed to just 6 inches by moving eight hinged struts when the craft was out of the water. It was built of plywood and covered with canvas and rubberized fabric. Its flat plywood bottom was reinforced with several wooden runners along its length, which allowed it to be dragged over rough ground without any damage. The two-man cockpit was covered with a watertight rubberized cover with two circular openings allowing access for the canoeists. The men were to wear camouflaged waterproof anoraks with elasticized bottoms that fitted snugly over the circular openings to prevent water entering the cockpit. A small breakwater on the foredeck helped deflect any water that hit the forward end of the craft.

A vital addition to the craft was a magnetic compass with luminous markings mounted just in front of the lead canoeist (navigating the cockles on the correct bearing in the dark was a vital aspect of the training programme). Propulsion was by means of long double-ended paddles. Each was made from two single paddles jointed at the centre point and designed so that one blade was at right angles to the other, so that when one blade was in the water thrusting the canoe forward, the other was at right angles to the motion producing little wind resistance.

The Cockle Mk II sat low in the water, making it particularly inconspicuous. However, when its crew were paddling at speed with their oars rising and dipping it became less so. If there was any danger of being observed by the enemy, the crew would split the paddles and continue with just a single paddle in use, crouching low in the cockpit to reduce their silhouette. With its very narrow sleek design and the smooth actions of very accomplished oarsmen, the Cockle Mk II could cut through the water swiftly, silently and hopefully almost unobserved.

By the end of October the final design of the Cockle Mk II had been agreed and the craft were in production. Now that the unit had its canoes the means of deploying them had to be developed. Launching a canoe at sea from a 'mother ship', most likely a submarine, was a difficult task. The very lightness of the canoe meant that when empty it did not sit well on the water. Trying to load stores and men into the flimsy craft as it rose and fell with the swell before it was swamped was fraught with danger. Ideally a method had to be devised to launch the cockle fully loaded with its cargo and crew straight into the sea.

An ingenious solution to the problem was developed by using the deck gun of a submarine as a crane. A long steel girder was clamped to the barrel of the gun from which a wood and canvas sling was attached. The fully loaded cockle, complete with its crew and stores, was placed into the sling and hoisted over the side and into the water. The sling's movement was controlled by means of the gun's transverse and elevation systems. Hasler's contribution to the design of the cockle had ensured that the craft had sufficient longitudinal strength to withstand the stresses of being hoisted fully loaded in this way.

By the last week in October Maj Hasler had devised a final scheme for the operation. He had obtained sufficient intelligence on the topography of the Gironde estuary, the River Garonne, the likely enemy defences, the state of the moon and tides, and on the location of the blockade busters in Bordeaux to build a workable plan. Aerial photographs and detailed maps showed the possible sites at which the canoes could hide during daylight hours and the stretches of river that could be navigated at night. The maps were colour-coded to show areas that were occupied by the enemy, those that might be dangerous and those that appeared to be safe.

The operation would be undertaken by six men in canoes, one officer (Hasler) and five other ranks selected from No. 1 Section of the RMBPD. It was believed that sufficient limpets for the destruction of six enemy ships could be carried in just three craft. The passage to the mouth of the Gironde would be by submarine and would take place in the dark phase of the moon at the beginning of December. The canoes would be launched soon after nightfall to allow the maximum time of darkness for them to pass the German seaward defences, the small naval base at Le Verdon and to enable them to get well into the river before daylight.

Maj Hasler and Capt Stewart put a Cockle Mk II through its paces in the calm seas of the Solent. Capt Stewart was Second-in-Command of the RMBPD and took charge of the unit while Hasler was in France during Operation *Frankton*. (Royal Marines Museum Collection)

Men of No. 1 Section RMBPD practise their rowing techniques in a whaler off Lumps Fort at Southsea. Several men who took part in Operation *Frankton* have since been identified: extreme left is Cpl Laver; immediately in front of Laver is Marine Ewart; extreme right is Sgt Wallace and behind Wallace, second from the right, is Cpl Sheard. (Royal Marines Museum Collection)

It was intended that the move upriver would take three days, with the attack on the blockade ships taking place on the evening of the fourth day. Each night, under the cover of darkness, the cockles would paddle their way upriver, covering between 15 and 20 miles per night. The state of the tides would mean that not all the night-time hours could be used effectively. If the current against them was too great they would have to seek shelter and wait for the tide to turn. Before light, a place for them to rest up would have to be located and the craft pulled out of the water and camouflaged. Once daylight came, the most nerve-wracking part of the journey had to be endured, for the men and their equipment would have to remain silent and unobserved throughout the whole of the day, possibly in fairly close proximity to the local population. The attack on the ships would take place in darkness during the early part of the evening so as to give the maximum time for the escape downriver before dawn. Each of the craft would plant limpets to a prearranged plan. After carrying out the attack, the cockles would move downstream to a point on the northern bank of the River Gironde, where the boats would be scuttled and their crews would make their escape.

Permission had been granted by the Royal Navy for the use of a submarine to carry Hasler's team to their launching point. However, there was one major drawback. The use of submarines was under strict control, as they were in demand for use by other units for covert operations or rendezvous. Hasler was told that his party could join HMS *Tuna* on the River Clyde in Scotland and disembark with the submarine on her next normal patrol in early December. As the patrol was destined for the North Atlantic, the route could be made via the Bay of Biscay to take in the requirements of Operation *Frankton*. There was, however, a particularly bad piece of news for Hasler to digest as well. He was told that it would be impossible for the submarine to return approximately a week later to pick up his group, as the risks were too great. By then the enemy defences would be on high alert looking for just such a rescue attempt. There was also a practical problem, for the chances of a submarine finding small dark canoes on a pitch-black night miles out to sea were negligible. Escape would have to made overland through Spain to Gibraltar.

Waiting and watching for any British attack around the River Gironde were troops of all three German services. This part of south-western France was garrisoned by the German 708th Division, a two-regiment static formation raised in the Strasbourg area in 1940. Two armed trawlers maintained a permanent patrol off the mouth of the river and were often joined by other trawlers on inshore minesweeping duties. Just inside the river on the south bank was the small port of Le Verdon, a base for a flotilla of six M-Class minesweepers. Most of the anti-aircraft defences in the area were manned by Luftwaffe personnel and these were grouped around the city of Bordeaux and at Le Verdon. Facing the sea to the south of Pointe de Grave were two medium coast defence batteries, one of six guns near Royannaiss and another emplacement of four guns closer to the lighthouse on the point. Several searchlight batteries covered the estuary and the first few miles of river upstream of Le Verdon. At Soulac-sur-Mer, four miles south of Pointe de Grave, was a seaward-facing radar station.

On 29 October Hasler's plan was put before the Executive Committee of COHQ in a meeting chaired by Lord Louis Mountbatten. The plan was approved unanimously with one major change; Mountbatten thought that the number of canoes should be increased from three to six in case of unforeseen accidents. The question of who was to command the raid was also raised. Mountbatten was reluctant to risk a senior officer crucial to the development of small boat tactics on such a dangerous operation. Hasler was reportedly distraught at the news and pleaded his case for going. He reasoned that he could never accurately develop raiding techniques and equipment if he had never participated in a raid. Moreover, he was loath to send his men on an operation without being there to guide them. 'If the raid was a failure,' he commented, 'how could I ever face the other men in the unit?' Mountbatten put the decision to the executive and sought the views of the other officers around the conference table. All except Col Neville felt that Hasler should not lead the raid because of his significance to his work with the BPB. Nonetheless Mountbatten, moved by Hasler's passion and commitment, relented. 'Against my better judgement,' he said with a smile, 'I'm going to let you go.'

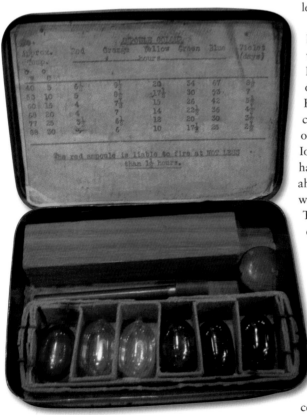

A box of coloured glass ampoules containing various concentrations of acetone of the type used in a limpet mine fuse during the raid. The strength of the liquid inside each ampoule determined the rate at which a celluloid washer in the mine's fusing mechanism would dissolve to release the spring-loaded firing pin and ignite the explosives. (Courtesy of Richard Wooldridge, Combined Military Services Museum)

A few days later final approval was granted by the Chiefs of Staff Committee when Hasler was already back in Scotland working with Lt Mackinnon and the No. 1 Section. They were on board the depot ship of the 3rd Submarine Flotilla anchored in Holy Loch, HMS *Forth*, carrying out their final training on the attack phase of the operation. The flotilla's commander, Capt Ionides, had already been informed that he would have the final say in whether the operation went ahead and Hasler had to prove to him that the unit was fully trained to fulfil the mission's objectives. The submarine carrying the party, HMS *Tuna*, was due to sail on her patrol on 30 November. By that time Ionides had to be convinced that the men were ready.

After No. 1 Section's arrival in Scotland on 30 October, training proceeded at an intense pace, with their departure for France planned for a month's time. Further training was dedicated to the use of the magnetic limpet mine. The mine was designed specifically for attachment to the sides of ships. Its 10lb of explosive was held in a metal canister mounted centrally on a metal frame. Attached to parallel bars alongside the frame were six 'horseshoe' magnets. The mine was designed to clamp itself on to the metal hull of the ship until the time set for it to explode. Its delayed-action fuses were chemically operated, with a striker pin held back by a dissolvable celluloid washer. Once the ampoule of acetone was broken inside the fuse, the washer would gradually dissolve over a prescribed period, eventually releasing the striker pin to detonate the explosive. The time taken for this was not exact and could be anywhere between four and eight hours, depending on the strength of the acetone and the temperature of the water. If several limpets were placed together there was also a danger that the first one to explode would dislodge the others and they would sink to the bottom to explode with no ill effects to the ship. To counter this, a secondary fuse was fitted, which was activated by two processes. First, it had to be armed by dissolving the water-soluble washer that guarded its detonator. This was achieved after an hour in the water. Second, its detonation was triggered in sympathy with the shock wave caused by another mine exploding on the same ship. In theory, one explosion would then set off all the limpet mines attached to the ship, but the fuse was still in its development stage and was not reliable.

To be effective the limpet mines had to be placed well below the waterline on the ship's sides. To accomplish this task, a placing rod was developed to facilitate the lowering of the mine into the water. The rod was a jointed steel pole 6ft long, capable of being disassembled and stored in the bottom of the canoe. The mine was hooked on to the end of the rod and lowered into the water before being pushed gently on to the ship's plates. But this delicate procedure would be complicated by the fact that it would be taking place in the tidal waters of the river and in all possibility with a current of several knots flowing past the canoe. To hold the craft on station during the placing of the mine, the second crewman would fasten on to the side of the ship by means of a magnetic hand-hold to keep the craft still.

To rehearse the placing of the limpet mines, Hasler's men had the assistance of the Dutch minesweeper *Jan Van Gelder*. On 4 November they practised attacking her with limpets while the ship steamed at a steady two knots to stimulate a tidal stream. Two days later they were at sea in the newly commissioned submarine P 339, HMS *Taurus*, trying out the makeshift mechanism and the procedure for launching the

NOVEMBER 9–15
1942

**Operation *Blanket*
takes place on the
Thames.**

A magnetic limpet mine preserved at the Combined Services Military Museum in Maldon, Essex. The thumb screw on the left of the mine unscrewed to allow an acetone ampoule to be inserted. Tightening the screw shattered the ampoule and allowed the acetone to come into contact with the celluloid washer holding back the firing pin. The orange fuses used in Operation *Frankton* allowed for a nine-hour delay. (Courtesy of Richard Wooldridge, Combined Military Services Museum)

Royal Marines inspect the large amount of kit required for a raid. This picture, showing men from the RMBPD, was taken at Southsea post-Operation *Frankton*. The canoe in the rear is a later three-man cockle. (Royal Marines Museum Collection)

cockles at sea. Both of these processes were run through again and again in the subsequent days until the section had fully mastered the techniques required.

On 9 November the party moved south to Margate in Kent. Hasler had organized a full-scale rehearsal of Operation *Frankton* to test his team. Operation *Blanket* had been devised to simulate the journey up the River Gironde to Bordeaux. The men of No. 1 Section were ordered to set off from Margate, paddle their way round to the mouth of the River Thames and then make their way 50 miles upriver to the London Docks unseen and undetected. The district naval commander had been warned of the exercise and the coast defences were all on the lookout for the canoes.

After two days of preparation and briefing, the cockles set out in darkness for their long journey to the ships tied up in the basins at Deptford. The exercise was not a success; right from the start things began to go wrong. Navigation was poor and the canoes soon lost sight of each other, meandering off course and into the open sea. After five nights the craft all arrived at Blackwall some three miles short of their objective, where the exercise was abandoned. All the men were exhausted and almost incapable of carrying on. Every canoe had been spotted on their way up the river and challenged at least twice. With the exercise an abject failure, the men of No. 1 Section were demoralized. On 15 November they were back at Southsea while Hasler attended a post-mortem on the failed operation at COHQ.

Four days later the whole team returned to Scotland together with the cockles ready to continue with the training programme. Hasler knew that he had only 11 days to iron out the causes of the failures identified during Operation *Blanket*. The rest of his team, including Lt Mackinnon, remained oblivious to the fact that they would be embarking on an operational sortie in a short amount of time.

One of the main reasons for the failure of Operation *Blanket* was navigation. The crews were not sufficiently skilled in calculating positions during periods of severe limitations. It took special expertise to keep station in a small canoe and plot a course while low in the water, in complete darkness, at the mercy of running tides and in appalling weather. This capability now had to be improved and all of No. 1 Section received special tuition from the Navigating Officer of HMS *Forth*.

After the exhaustions of the exercise up the River Thames, physical fitness was back on the agenda with route marches over the nearby hills, as well as weapons handling and stealth technique training. There was also further familiarization with the placing of limpet mines and the drills required to fuse them. Arming this explosive device required complete concentration and the team practised the method by numbered stages until all could accomplish the task blindfolded. Hasler was well aware that he was pushing the men hard, especially when they were still in the dark regarding the planned operation.

After a week back in Scotland Hasler decided to grant the men a break from the pressurized rounds of training. He called them together and announced that they all had shore leave for one night, to use and abuse as they thought fit. There was just one proviso: they all had to be ready and fit for duty in the morning.

THE RAID

The submarine that had been allocated by 3rd Submarine Flotilla for Operation *Frankton*, HMS *Tuna*, berthed alongside the support ship HMS *Forth* on 25 November. Hasler and his team could now familiarize themselves with the crew and the vessel that would take them to France.

HMS *Tuna* was commanded by Lt Richard Raikes. She was a T-Class submarine with the pennant number N94. The vessel had been launched on 10 May 1940 and had been commanded by Lt Raikes since 24 August 1942. The submarine had a number of kills to its credit during two years of patrols: the German merchant ship *Tirrana* (ex Norwegian), the German *Ostmark* and the French tug *Chaissiron* had all been sunk by *Tuna*. Earlier that year, on 10 March, Raikes, then in command of the patrolling S-Class submarine HMS *Seawolf*, had sighted the German battleship *Tirpitz*. Though his submarine was too far away to engage *Tirpitz*, his enemy-locating report enabled the carrier *Victorious* to attack the enemy capital ship with her Albacore torpedo-bombers.

Lt Raikes received his final operational orders for *Frankton* on 26 November, detailing the timings and objectives of the raid. HMS *Tuna* would sail on 30 November for a normal patrol in the Bay of Biscay with Hasler's party. *Tuna* was ordered to attack at all times if any enemy forces were encountered. If such an attack were to prejudice the successful implementation of *Frankton*, then the operation should be considered cancelled.

It was essential that the raid be conducted at a time of 'no moon'. During this period the first possible night was 5/6 December and the last possible night was 12/13 December. Raikes was ordered to disembark the Royal Marine party with their canoes off the mouth of the River Gironde at a position just south of the minefield laid by the RAF. The actual night chosen would depend on a number of factors, the most important of which was the state of the weather. It was also vital to release the cockles so that they would enter the Gironde during a period of slack water. It would be impossible for the canoes to be paddled into the mouth of the river against an ebb tide.

HMS *Tuna* (Pennant No. N94) lying inside the submarine HMS *Tigris* (Pennant No. N63) at Holy Loch. Both submarines are tied up next to their supply ship HMS *Forth* readying themselves for their next operational voyages. HMS *Tigris* was later stationed in the Mediterranean where she was sunk in February 1943 by the German submarine chaser *UJ2210*. (IWM A6586)

**NOVEMBER 30
1942**

**HMS *Tuna* sails
out of Holy Loch.**

During the last few days of November 1942, time was spent by the men of No. 1 Section finalizing their training and preparing for an operation. The method of stowing cockles inside the submarine and disembarking them through the forward hatch was now practised in HMS *Tuna*. The compasses in the canoes were checked for deviation, while the cockles were fully loaded with their complete stores and sets of limpet mines. The marines familiarized themselves with the stowage of these stores and equipment inside the cockles so that even in the dark they could locate any item that they needed. Further practice also took place on the fusing and setting of limpet mines until this could be done quickly and confidently, almost without thought. In addition the cockles received their final coat of camouflage paint, a scheme of dark-green and black irregular patterns and shapes.

The six canoes had been given names beginning with 'C' and organized into two divisions. Division A contained *Catfish* with Maj Hasler and Marine Sparks, *Crayfish* crewed by Cpl Laver and Marine Mills, and *Conger* with Corporal Sheard and Marine Moffat. Division B comprised *Cuttlefish* containing Lt Mackinnon and Marine Conway, *Coalfish* with Sgt Wallace and Marine Ewart, and finally *Cachalot* with Marine Ellery and Marine Fisher.

By this time Lt Mackinnon was well aware that an operation was imminent, although he had no knowledge of where the target was or what was involved. The men had also heard rumours that something was in the air and as the date for departure drew near it became increasingly obvious. The final clue was the order to sew on to the sleeves of their clothing their badges of rank: the Royal Marine shoulder flashes and Commando badge showing an anchor, a rifle and a set of wings.

The Sea Voyage

On the morning of 30 November, Maj Hasler and his team of 13 men – Marine Norman Colley was embarked with the rest of No. 1 Section as a 'spare man' should anyone have to drop out – all boarded HMS *Tuna* and settled into their quarters. At 1030 hours the submarine slipped away from its parent ship HMS *Forth* and eased out of Holy Loch into the River Clyde. Once clear of the river the submarine turned to starboard and made for the Inchmarnock exercise area between the Isle of Arran and the mainland. Here in sheltered waters Lt Raikes stopped his submarine and allowed the crews to practise embarking the cockles. Two separate hoists were made with all of the fully loaded canoes. Finally, one more swinging of each boat's compasses was made to take account of the metal from the stowed limpet mines and other metal stores. From this exercise Raikes was able to determine that it would be likely that the whole operation of disembarking the cockles would take just under an hour to complete while at sea without damage to the canoes.

That evening as the submarine motored south Hasler called all his men together and finally gave them details of the raid they were to undertake. When it was revealed that the target was German shipping tied up in the port of Bordeaux 60 miles from the sea, they immediately recognized its similarity to Operation *Blanket* in the Thames some weeks previously. They agreed that it was a task well within their means to accomplish successfully. Maj Hasler also gave an overview of the operation using maps and aerial photographs. The only aspect of the forthcoming operation that dampened their enthusiasm was the planned overland escape via Spain. The thought of travelling hundreds of miles through territory occupied by any number of people hostile to their cause, not to mention the enemy soldiers in control of the region, unsurprisingly caused some disquiet. Each man was to be issued with a bag containing escape equipment including a compass and some local currency but Hasler

**DECEMBER 6
1942**

**Arriving at the
Gironde estuary,
Lt Raikes delays
Operation
Frankton for 24
hours.**

A Cockle Mk I being manoeuvred down the torpedo hatch of a submarine. One of the most important parameters of the newer Cockle Mk II that Hasler helped to design was that it had to be able to pass through this hatch unhindered. During the operation, the canoe manned by Marines Ellery and Fisher snagged on some protrusion while coming through the hatch and was damaged to such an extent that it could not take part in the attack. (IWM MH 227515)

stressed that each crew must move in pairs independently of the others. Two men together would be less conspicuous; any more and the party would attract notice from the locals as well as the security forces. Arrangements for their escape had been made with the French Resistance, with each two-man crew having to make their way approximately 100 miles north to the small town of Ruffec, where a lookout from the Resistance would be waiting for their arrival. The men would then be handed over to the established escape organization that ran across the country to the Spanish border, organized by the enigmatic 'Marie-Claire'.

Lt Richard Raikes, commander of the submarine HMS *Tuna*. The 30-year-old Raikes had previously commanded the submarine HMS *Seawolf* before taking over HMS *Tuna* and was later attached to the staff of the RAF Coastal Command. At the end of the war Raikes took part in Operation *Deadlight*, the scuttling of over 100 captured German U-boats in the waters to the north of Ireland. (IWM A14400)

To add to their concerns none of the men, with the exception of Hasler, spoke French. Naturally Hasler offered the men the opportunity to drop out but it was always unlikely that anyone would take him up on the offer after such intensive training.

Over the coming days of voyage, Hasler went into further detail with every man to ensure that they were familiar with every aspect of the operation. From leaving the submarine until inside the estuary, the two divisions would move as one group, with A Division leading in an arrowhead formation followed by B Division, also in an arrowhead. Once inside the river Hasler would determine which side of the waterway would be taken for the first lying-up place. At some point after this he would also give final instructions to the CO of B Division (Lt Mackinnon), who would then proceed independently with his three canoes for the rest of the operation. Hasler stressed that if any canoe became separated from its party, then it was to carry on with the mission – alone, if necessary. Furthermore, if any cockle got into difficulties that would compromise the operation then it was to be scuttled and its crew left to make their own escape.

Hasler made it clear that the primary objective of the raid was to attack the largest of the merchant ships found in the harbour. The secondary objectives were to attack tankers and any lesser merchant targets of opportunity. Once the canoes had arrived in the port, the crews were to attack the enemy ships in three areas: Bordeaux west bank, Bordeaux east bank and Bassens North and South, which were located just downstream from the main harbour. To ensure that there was no duplication of effort, one boat from each division was to attack in each of these areas, with A Division's cockles placing their limpets on the upstream side of enemy ships, while the crews of B Division attached their mines to the downstream sides.

There were a few notes of caution for the men. If the submarine was surprised on the surface by the enemy during the embarkation process and its commander thought it necessary to dive, those cockles already launched would continue with the operation independently. In view of the possible danger, Maj Hasler's canoe was the first to be floated clear, followed by Lt Mackinnon's and then those of the NCOs. Hasler outlined the enemy forces that might be encountered: two armed trawlers patrolling the estuary; coast defences either side of the mouth of the river; searchlight batteries on the coast and alongside German flak batteries; up to six minesweepers and escort vessels based at Le Verdon; and a number of lighter motor craft moving up and down the river. There might also be the chance of U-boats moving to and from their base at Bordeaux. Wherever possible the canoes were to move inshore of the buoyed channel mid-river where most of this traffic was likely to be encountered.

Finally there was also the danger of observation from the air as there were three German airfields in the locality, at Hourtain, Bordeaux and Royan. During daylight hours, it was imperative that the crews remained motionless and their boats were well camouflaged. As HMS *Tuna* journeyed south, the RMBPD pored over charts and aerial photographs of the Gironde and the final approaches to Bordeaux up the River Garonne. Colour-coded maps were distributed, which showed which stretches of the river were likely to pose a risk from enemy forces and which were expected to be safe. Some simple instructions in the basics of the French language were taught by Hasler to give the men a chance of making contact with the civilian population. The intricacies of the Number 3 code used by downed airmen and POW escapees were also explained. This imaginative method of sending signals back to England via the French Resistance would let the authorities at home know of the success or otherwise of the raid and inform them who was alive and free in occupied territory.

During the afternoon of Sunday 6 December Lt Raikes brought HMS *Tuna* to the area south of the Gironde estuary and surfaced to periscope depth. He knew at least that he was clear of both the minefield sown by the RAF and those of the enemy, but he had to get a visual fix to establish his exact position before releasing Hasler's party. The sky was overcast and the sea was smooth with just a slight swell. Raikes was concerned that his periscope would leave a long trail across the flat calm of the ocean, which would be easily spotted by fishing vessels and other craft in the area, but he was compelled to creep up the coast to search the shoreline for some identifiable features that would help determine his exact position.

The land was completely devoid of anything that Raikes could recognize; all that was visible was a featureless line of pine trees and sand dunes, occasionally broken by a small village with a nondescript church spire. His vessel could be close to the minefields or miles to the south, it was impossible to tell. After some time creeping along the coast Raikes realized that he was risking the operation, as every minute he motored northwards brought him closer to the minefields. He dived below periscope depth and eased his vessel out to sea. The operation would have to be delayed by 24 hours and he would have to try again later that night to get a fix by the stars. He later explained his predicament in his after-action report: 'The night of the 6/7 proved impossible, as I was completely unable to establish my position with sufficient certainty and it was imperative to be dead accurate. This was unfortunate as conditions were quite perfect, a nice mist coming down immediately after dark.'

Just before dawn on the 7th, the submarine surfaced and Raikes was able to get a good star fix on his position. He dived again and began working his vessel slowly north so that by 1345 hours he was able to get an accurate visual fix. There were a number of fishing boats in the area and Raikes used his periscope sparingly to avoid his presence being reported to the enemy. There was also a danger from above: 'Air activity by ME 110s, ME 109s, JU 88s and Dornier 18s throughout the day was intense,' he was later to write. 'The surface was oily calm with a long swell.' It looked as though all would be well for the release of the canoes that night and Hasler was given the good news.

Just after nightfall, at 1800 hours, a German armed trawler was spotted patrolling along a line north-west to south-east, right through the intended position for disembarkation. Raikes decided to release the cockles a little closer to the shore, nearer the RAF's minefield than he had originally intended. He was now confident that his position would be 'dead accurate'. Hasler was delighted with the new site for disembarkation as it was closer to the shore and nearer the mouth of the estuary. But Raikes still had some doubts about his decision: 'I don't think those mines could have been laid in a more embarrassing position,' he later recorded, 'as they seemed to interfere with every possible plan of action from the very start. This plan quite evidently required extreme accuracy in navigation even allowing for the touching faith of the authorities in the accuracy of the positions given by the RAF – a faith which I did not share.'

At 1917 hours, Raikes brought his submarine to the surface in position 45° 22' N – 1° 14'W, around four miles off the coast. He swept the horizon through a cold

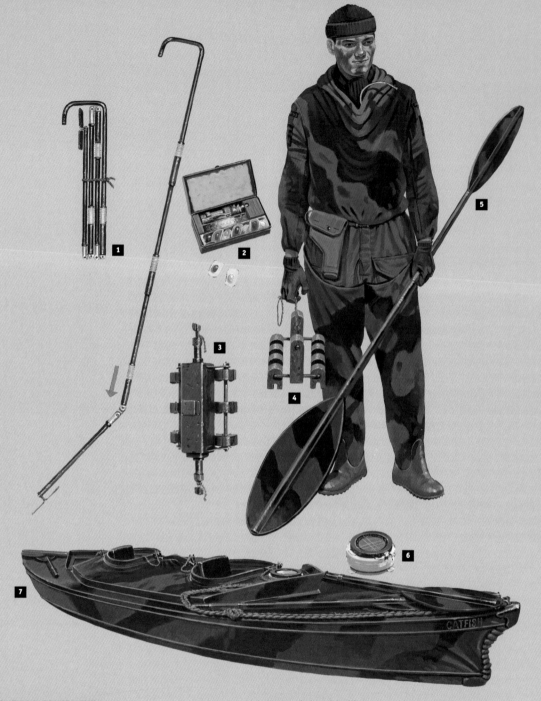

WEAPONS AND EQUIPMENT

1 Placing rod for limpet mines (collapsed and extended)
2 Fuse box for limpet mines
3 Limpet mine

4 Magnetic hand-hold
5 Two-part paddle (connected)
6 Magnetic compass
7 Cockle MK II

One of the raiders from the Royal Marine Boom Patrol Detachment dressed and equipped for the raid. Underneath his external clothing he wears normal battledress. His all–weather anorak jacket is designed with an elasticated waist to fit over the circular opening in the cockle to make the cockpit watertight. His waders and boots are welded together in one piece to make them waterproof. The items shown around him were for the offensive part of the mission. Also carried in the canoe during the raid were sufficient supplies of water and food as well as maps, photographs and escape equipment.

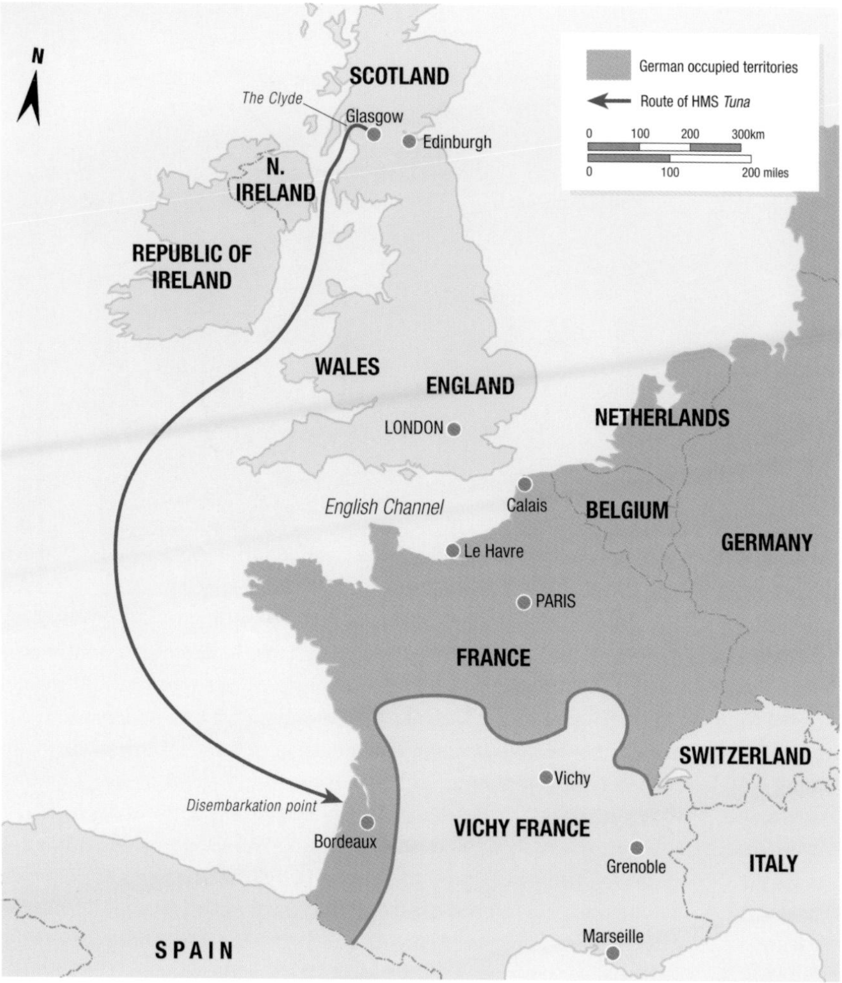

The route of HMS *Tuna*.

1917 hours
Raikes gives the go-
ahead for the raid
to begin.

DECEMBER 8
1942

0545 hours
Coalfish is lost, Sgt
Wallace and Marine
Ewart surrender to
the Luftwaffe.

clear night to look for danger and saw that the enemy trawler was four miles further away out to sea. He was confident that his submarine was invisible to it, a dark outline against the dark shore. Everything else was clear, the sea a flat calm. Raikes called Hasler up to the conning tower and gave him the good news: disembarkation could proceed as planned. Raikes asked the Royal Marine officer, 'Are you happy to go?' 'Yes,' replied Hasler. They shook hands and wished each other luck. There was no turning back now.

One by one the cockles were brought out of the submarine through the forward hatch and lined up on deck. The last to come up was Hasler's canoe, *Catfish*, which was placed underneath the submarine's deck guns so as to be first on the hoist and first into the water. Final preparations were made to the cockles, buoyancy bags inflated and the last of the stores loaded. During the process a major problem was discovered. The fabric of *Cachalot* was torn as it came through the hatch and the subsequent damage made it impossible for the boat to continue with the raid. With a heavy heart Hasler informed Marines Ellery and Fisher that they would be left behind. Operation *Frankton* had suffered its first casualty, reducing the raiding party to just five canoes.

A few miles to the north-east, just north of Pointe de la Négade, the German radar station W310 at Soulac-sur-Mer was monitoring the approaches to the

The crew of the QF 4-inch gun onboard HMS *Tuna* during a training session. It was this gun that was used as a hoist to lift the fully loaded cockles into the sea during Operation *Frankton*. (IWM D12466)

Gironde estuary and beyond. As HMS *Tuna* surfaced, her sudden appearance was immediately spotted by enemy RDF operators and her presence reported to Kapitän zur See Max Gebauner, German Sea Defence Commandant Gascony. Gebauner was at that very moment at his headquarters in Royan just across the mouth of the river, dining with German Naval Commander-in-Chief Western France, Admiral Johannes Bachmann. The admiral was in Royan prior to inspecting four of Gebauner's Chasseur-type submarine-chasers the next day, which were then lying at anchor across the estuary off Le Verdon. When news of the British submarine's appearance was given to Gebauner, he ordered the coast defences batteries to be alerted and for all searchlight batteries to switch on their lights and sweep the area of the sea off the coast. All Hasler's boats were out on the upper deck of the submarine by 1945 hours. Raikes trimmed down his vessel to ease the launching process and the cockles began to be lowered gently into the sea complete with their crews and all stores. Just as Hasler's craft was suspended in the slings ready to be swung out, a searchlight on the coast near Pointe de la Négade came on and began sweeping across the still waters. Then another burst into life and then another until all the enemy's lights on that stretch of the coast were fully illuminated. Raikes was still confident that the trimmed-down silhouette of his submarine could not be seen, but the sweeping lights gave a keener sense of urgency to the disembarkation process. A short while later Raikes was told by his lookout that it seemed as though the armed trawler had been informed by the shore battery that something was afoot and was now closing on the submarine.

Lt Bull, the deck officer controlling the launching of the cockles, remained outwardly unperturbed as he quietly and efficiently continued organizing the lowering of each boat into the water. After 25 minutes the torturous process was complete. Maj Hasler brought all of his canoes into formation, waved goodbye to the conning tower and made for the shore. Lt Raikes watched as the small craft were swallowed up by the dark night. 'At 2020 hours I waved "au revoir" to a magnificent bunch of black faced villains with whom it has been a real pleasure to work, and, withdrew to the south and west,' wrote the submarine's commander in his report. The five cockles were on their own.

The Journey Upriver

Maj Hasler led his five cockles in formation through a calm sea towards the mouth of the Gironde. There was still some 10 miles to negotiate before they entered the river. The clear December night had brought the temperature down to near freezing, but regular paddle strokes gradually warmed up the marines and loosened muscles that had stiffened in the cramped conditions of the submarines. Hasler steered the group to a point two miles west of Pointe de la Négade and after three and a half hours of paddling, with five-minute rests each hour, at 2350 hours the cockles passed over some turbulence caused by the shallows of the Banc des Olives. The steep rollers caused by the ground swell had been marked on their navigation maps and were negotiated without any problems.

Once clear of the shallows, Hasler moved his little fleet nearer to land and proceeded northwards closer to the shore. 'We followed the line of the coast, now clearly visible about a mile and a half away,' wrote the major in his after-action report. 'Shortly afterwards the sound of broken water ahead indicated a tidal race. This came as an unpleasant surprise, not having been apparent from the chart or the Sailing Directions. Owing to the strength of the stream there was no chance of avoiding the race, which proved to be quite severe for such small craft.'

A natural occurrence formed when a fast-moving tide passes through a constriction such as a narrow channel, the tidal race produced a stretch of broken water with strong swirling undercurrents and waves 4–5ft high. The Cockle Mk II was well able to weather this provided it crested each wave and the cockpit cover was securely fastened, but the men had not been trained to tackle this sort of unexpected obstacle. There was nothing for it but to plod ahead through the maelstrom, using the paddles to keep the boat head on into the waves.

Hasler's canoe was first through the disturbance to emerge into calmer water. He kept station waiting for the others to catch up. One by one they reported through and gathered around his craft. A quick head count found that *Coalfish* containing Sgt Wallace and Marine Ewart was missing. The canoes spread out to look for it but there was no sign of the cockle on the now still water. Hasler reasoned that since both men and the boat had buoyancy equipment, it was possible that the craft had not capsized but had turned further inshore when they found themselves separated from the group. Hasler knew nothing more could be done to find the missing cockle. He called all the boats back into formation and once again set course for the Gironde estuary. Operation *Frankton* was now down to just four canoes.

Coalfish had indeed survived the tidal race, but Sgt Wallace and Marine Ewart's craft was now well out of position and close to shore. The two marines had lost direction and were confused, but they carried on with the operation, continuing as

The Cockles and their Crews

Catfish	Maj Hasler and Marine Sparks	Target: Bordeaux West Bank
Cuttlefish	Lt Mackinnon and Marine Conway	Target: Bordeaux West Bank
Crayfish	Cpl Laver and Marine Mills	Target: Bordeaux East Bank
Coalfish	Sgt Wallace and Marine Ewart	Target: Bordeaux East Bank
Conger	Cpl Sheard and Marine Moffat	Target: Bassens North and South
Cachalot	Marine Fisher and Marine Ellery	Target: Bassens North and South

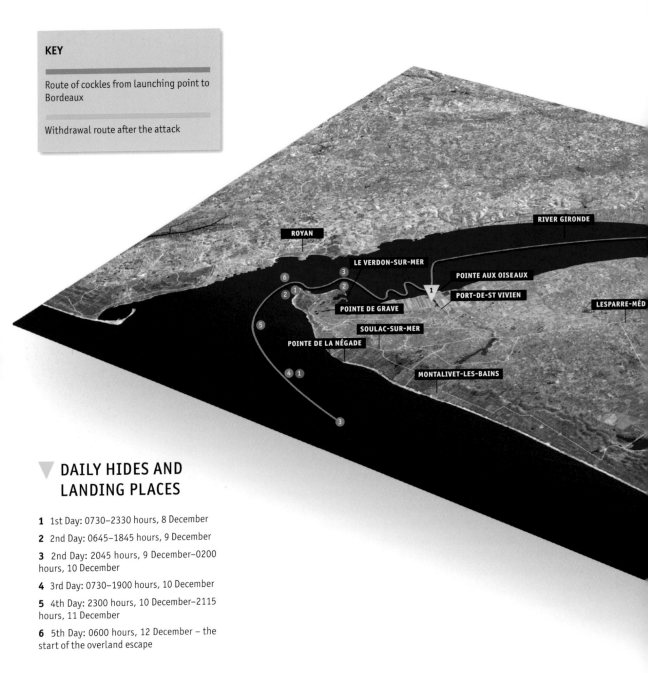

KEY

Route of cockles from launching point to Bordeaux

Withdrawal route after the attack

ROYAN

LE VERDON-SUR-MER

RIVER GIRONDE

POINTE AUX OISEAUX

POINTE DE GRAVE

PORT-DE-ST VIVIEN

LESPARRE-MÉD

SOULAC-SUR-MER

POINTE DE LA NÉGADE

MONTALIVET-LES-BAINS

▼ DAILY HIDES AND LANDING PLACES

1 1st Day: 0730–2330 hours, 8 December

2 2nd Day: 0645–1845 hours, 9 December

3 2nd Day: 2045 hours, 9 December–0200 hours, 10 December

4 3rd Day: 0730–1900 hours, 10 December

5 4th Day: 2300 hours, 10 December–2115 hours, 11 December

6 5th Day: 0600 hours, 12 December – the start of the overland escape

EVENTS ❶ – ❻

1 Pointe de Grave lighthouse

2 German inshore naval base at Le Verdon-sur-Mer

3 Launching point from HMS Tuna (2022 hours, 7 December)

4 First tidal race

5 Second tidal race

6 Third tidal race

THE LOSS OF THE COCKLES ❶ – ❹

1 *Coalfish* – Wallace and Ewart lost

2 *Conger* – Sheard and Moffat lost

3 *Cuttlefish* – Mackinnon and Conway separated

4 *Cuttlefish* – Mackinnon and Conway's cockle sunk off Bec d'Ambès

THE APPROACH: THE COCKLES' ROUTE UP THE RIVER GARONNE

8–12 DECEMBER 1942

At 2020 hours on 7th December 1942, the submarine HMS *Tuna* launched five small cockles onto a hostile sea off the French coast. So began an epic journey for their Royal Marine crews which led them up the Gironde and Garonne Rivers towards their target. The operation involved five long days of cramped hiding places and five exhausting nights of paddling before they reached their goal and finally confronted the German blockade busters moored along the supposedly safe quays at Bordeaux.

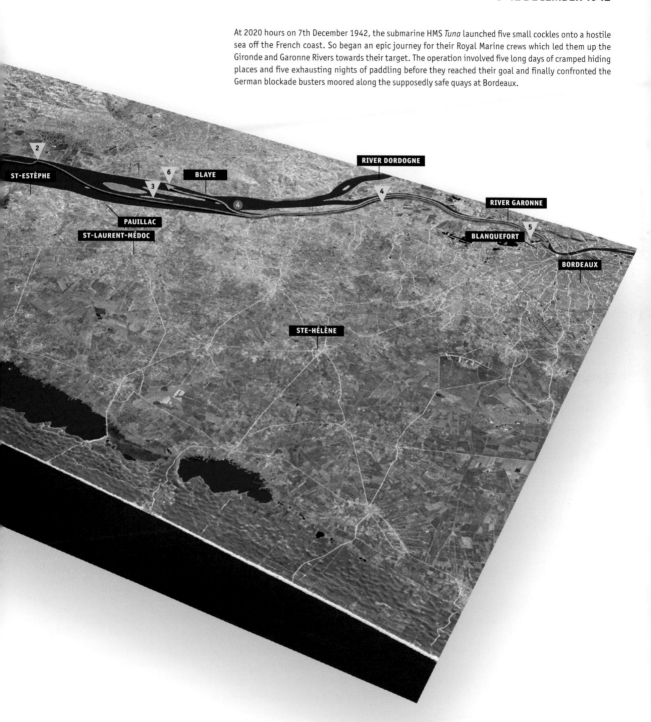

ST-ESTÈPHE
2
6 BLAYE
3
4
PAUILLAC
ST-LAURENT-MÉDOC
RIVER DORDOGNE
RIVER GARONNE
4
5
BLANQUEFORT
BORDEAUX
STE-HÉLÈNE

An original Cockle Mk II, now preserved in the Combined Military Services Museum at Maldon in Essex. The canoe on display has been identified as being one from the batch constructed by SARO for use by the RMBPD and recent research shows that it is most likely the cockle *Cachalot*, which was damaged while being passed through the hatch onboard HMS *Tuna* during the raid. (Courtesy of Richard Wooldridge, Combined Military Services Museum)

best they could towards the Gironde estuary. Sometime later that night their canoe was swept inshore and swamped, most likely by another tidal race. The two men were tipped into the sea and had to swim for shore, making landfall in an exhausted and dispirited state near Pointe de Grave. Hasler and the remaining cockles had meanwhile paddled on towards the estuary of the Gironde. A short while after being hit by the first tidal race they were hit again. Another rush of broken water, even stronger than the first, loomed up out of the night and plunged the canoes into another swirling nightmare. Great walls of water crashed over the boats and it took all the muscle power available to each man to try to keep the prow of his craft head on to the running sea. Within a few minutes the leading cockle was through. As Hasler emerged on the far side he took a roll call and found that *Conger* had capsized, throwing Cpl Sheard and Marine Moffat into the icy water. The buoyancy bags kept the cockle afloat, but despite the best efforts of the men in the other canoes it proved impossible to bale out the flooded craft.

Hasler now had a serious problem. The men in the water could not be taken aboard any of the other craft and they were already suffering the effects of the cold sea. The major knew that they were likely to die of exposure if they were left in the water for too long. He later described what happened next: 'An effort was made to tow the two swimmers somewhat further inshore. During this proceeding the tide had carried the party round the Pointe de Grave, more than a quarter mile off shore, and through a third, but less violent, tide race. The lighthouse on the point had been switched on at full strength and lit up the scene quite brilliantly for a time.' Fortunately, although bathed periodically in its dazzling white beam of the light, they were not seen by the enemy.

They were now just inside the estuary and the task of towing the men through the water was slowing down the whole enterprise. Hasler felt that he had done all he could; it was now time to let them go. He explained the situation to the two unfortunate marines, wished them good luck and told them to make for the shore, believing that the tide would carry them close to the mole at Le Verdon.

Once adrift from the main party, the tide did indeed carry the two men towards the shore, but they both succumbed to exposure before reaching it. Their lifeless bodies swirled around in the eddying currents and were eventually swept back out to sea on the next tide. Days later the body of Marine Moffat was found on a beach 50

miles to the north at Sables d'Olonne. No trace of Cpl Sheard was ever found. Operation *Frankton* was now down to just three canoes.

The setbacks had compromised Hasler's timetable and he now knew that there was not enough time to make it across the river to his preferred route along the east bank that night. Worse still, the tide had carried them close into the western shore and was taking them dangerously near the tiny port of Le Verdon. Ahead he could see the long mole jutting out into the river and knew that it was probably guarded by sentries. Hasler now struggled in the fast-flowing tide to bring the three remaining craft away from the mole, and as he did so he was surprised to see the shapes of several much larger naval vessels anchored in a line ahead of him. The party had almost run into Kapitän zur See Max Gebauner's four inshore vessels, which were lined up ready for inspection that day by Admiral Bachmann.

Hasler called his three canoes together and pointed out the problems. They would have to pass between the German warships and the mole, all of which could well have lookouts scanning the river. He proposed that they should go through this defile singly, separated by several hundred yards, using only single paddles and keeping as low a profile as possible. *Catfish* would lead the way, followed by *Crayfish* and then Lt Mackinnon's *Cuttlefish*.

The first two cockles negotiated the danger zone without incident, joining together once they were clear of the threat. There was some activity on one of the German ships as Hasler's canoe passed through and for a short moment a signal lamp began winking out a message to the shore, but nothing untoward happened to make them think they had been spotted. Further upstream the two craft paused for the third boat to meet up with them. They waited and waited, but there was no sign of *Cuttlefish*. It looked as though Mackinnon's boat had lost formation and passed the other two craft further out on the river. While they waited they thought they heard a shout and it was later suggested that a shot had been fired, but there was no sign of alarm on the river, which led Hasler to believe that Lt Mackinnon had been seen. He was sure that the young lieutenant was somewhere out on the river and would proceed with the operation alone. Hasler's group was now down to just two cockles.

Once clear of Le Verdon, the four Royal Marines set course down the west bank, keeping a careful check on the time to ensure that the two canoes reached their initial hide, wherever it might be, well before daylight. Their first attempt to land at around

The site of Maj Hasler's first daytime hide at Pointe dux Oiseaux on the left bank of the River Gironde. The exit of the small creek that leads up to the fishing village of St Vivian can be seen on the right. The state of the tides shows the three-quarters of a mile of sandy mud over which the canoes had to be dragged on the second night of the raid. (Ken Ford)

KOMMANDOBEFEHL: HITLER'S 'KILL COMMANDOS' ORDER

In October 1942 Hitler issued his notorious order for the execution of all British special forces personnel captured during raids. He was acting in response to reports reaching him that during a commando attack on the island of Sark, five German prisoners had been bound and killed by the raiders. Further reports later informed him that during the Dieppe raid in August 1942, Canadians had also tied the hands of a number of Germans who were later found dead. It was later thought that the Germans had been tied up as prisoners and had been killed by cross-fire during the raids and not shot out of hand by the raiders themselves. Nonetheless, Hitler was incensed by these reports and decided that this underhand and brutal treatment of German prisoners by what he called 'saboteurs' had to be ruthlessly punished. The order was kept as secret as possible, even though it was disseminated down the chain of command, so no written copies were to be kept. It was issued in a limited number of controlled copies, each of which was prefaced with a covering note: 'After verbal distribution to subordinate sections the above authorities must hand this order over to the next highest section which is responsible for its confiscation and destruction.'

The Führer

No. 003830/42g MOST SECRET/OWK/West   Führer's Headquarters, 18.10.1942

1 For some time now our opponents have used methods of warfare, which are contrary to the International Agreement of Geneva. Especially brutal and underhand behaviour is shown by the so-called Commandos who, it has been proved, have been recruited partly from released criminals in enemy countries. Captured orders yield the information that the Commandos are ordered not only to obtain prisoners but also to kill defenceless prisoners the moment they may hinder the execution of their purpose or create any other hindrance. At last orders have been found which definitely state that the annihilation of prisoners is required.

2 Consequently it has been declared in an Appendix to the Armed Forces Report that in future Germany will employ the same principle against British sabotage units and those of Britain's allies. That is, wherever they operate they must be ruthlessly annihilated in battle by German troops.

3 I therefore order:

   From now on in all so-called Commando operations in Europe or Africa all enemies attacked by German troops, even if it is apparently a question of soldiers in uniform or shock troops with or without arms, must be annihilated to the last man, in battle or in flight. It makes no difference whether they are landed by sea or air or dropped by parachute for these operations. Even if those particular troops, when discovered, should make attempts to surrender, any pardon is to be refused. Concerning this, the OKW Supreme Command of the Armed Forces must be notified by a detailed report in the Armed Forces communiqué, in each individual case.

4 If individual members of these Commandos should fall into the hands of the Armed Forces in a different way, as agents, saboteurs, etc. – for instance through the police force in countries occupied by us – then they must be immediately handed over to the SD (Security Services). Any custody under military protection, e.g. P.O.W. camps, etc., even if it is only a transitory measure, is strictly prohibited.

5 These instructions do not apply to the treatment of those soldiers who are taken prisoner or surrender during normal battles (large-scale attacks, large-scale landings and air-landing operations). Neither do these instructions apply to those enemy soldiers who fall into are hands after sea battles, or those who, after air battles, endeavour to save their lives by parachute.

6 I shall make all commanders and officers answerable by court martial for omitting to carry out this order, either if they have neglected their duty in giving these instructions to their units, or if they act contrary to these instructions.

Signed   Adolf HITLER

0630 hours resulted in failure. As they approached the shore their way was barred by a shingle bank topped by a line of stakes. The next attempt some time later was more successful. A small promontory jutted out into the Gironde and, on the small patch of sand that formed the beach, the tired, wet cold raiders eased their aching bodies out of their cramped cockles and collapsed from sheer exhaustion. They had paddled their way over 23 nautical miles that night and endured the rough seas of three tide races. They deserved their rest that cold December morning.

Hasler, however, soon had them on their feet and hauling the cockles across the sand above the high water mark into some low scrub that lined the river bank. Camouflage nets were placed over the canoes to conceal them just as daylight was breaking. The party had come to rest alongside the Pointe aux Oiseaux and just behind this headland was a small river that led up to the fishing village of St Vivien. The River Gironde here was extremely wide and this stretch of its western side was lined by a high man-made embankment, which served as a dyke. This helped to conceal the hiding place of the canoes from traffic moving parallel to the shore along the quiet road that followed the length of the dyke.

A few hours earlier Wallace and Ewart had also come ashore, exhausted from their ordeal in the water. There was no possibility of continuing with the operation, for their capsized cockle *Coalfish* was being tumbled around in the high surf spewing its contents along the shoreline. They had nothing with them but the clothes on their backs and it seemed clear to them that it would be impossible to make their way to Spain without their carefully packed escape gear. For them the war was over and they decided to give themselves up and become prisoners of war.

The two men had come ashore near the Pointe de Grave in the sector guarded by German 708 Division. The wide sandy coastline was devoid of civilians but widely occupied by scattered enemy emplacements. It was not long before they came across a Luftwaffe anti-aircraft battery. The marines were taken prisoner by the flak personnel at 0545 hours and they explained that they were shipwrecked English sailors, but their painted faces, camouflaged anoraks and Combined Operations badges showed them to be something quite different. The prisoners were taken to the Luftwaffe sick bay near the Pointe de Grave lighthouse and the local commander of Flak Detachment 595 passed on news of the arrests to Kapitän zur See Max Gebauner in Royan, who, at around 0800 hours, forwarded it to Naval Command Bordeaux. The Luftwaffe declined responsibility for the shipwrecked men and suggested they be transferred to the naval prisoner's camp at Fallingbostel. In the meantime the naval Commander-in-Chief West, Admiral Bachmann, was also informed.

Later that day Admiral Bachmann sent a signal to Naval War Staff in Paris outlining events thus far and made it clear that they were no ordinary sailors. They were in his opinion in France to carry out a sabotage operation. The signal explained that in the course of the day many items were found on the shore: 'Explosive charges with adhesive magnets, chart material of the Gironde estuary, aerial photographs of Bordeaux harbour installations, camouflage material and provisions for several days. Surgeon of the ferry flak states that the prisoners' faces were painted green and they had arrived soaked through. Footprints discovered led one to conclude that a landing was made off the area of the unoccupied Verdon battery. A collapsible boat was observed but salvage was not possible. Investigation as to whether further men had landed has been put in motion.' As commandos the two prisoners should have been subject to Hitler's Secret Order of 18 October 1942, meaning immediate delivery to Sicherheitsdienst (SD), the intelligence service of the SS, for execution. But Admiral Bachmann was inclined to interrogate them first to find out more about their mission.

During the morning Bachmann ordered the immediate questioning of Wallace and

DECEMBER 8 1942

0630 hours Maj Hasler's remaining two canoes land on the banks of the River Gironde.

DECEMBER 8/9 1942

After paddling though the night, Hasler's crews lie up opposite St Estéphe.

Ewart by the SD in Bordeaux, but the SS there refused as this was expressly forbidden. Hitler had specifically ordered that 'saboteurs must be annihilated to the last man immediately they are caught'. Any officer who defied this order was liable to face a court martial. Bachmann was adamant that they should first be questioned about their mission and so had Wallace and Ewart transferred across the Gironde to the old naval fort at Royan under naval supervision. He wanted to know what they had landed from and whether any other troops had also landed, if so, where, how many and what was their mission? To cover himself with Naval High Command and ultimately Hitler himself, in his signal he added, 'on conclusion of interrogation, if previous findings are confirmed, I have ordered immediate shooting on account of attempted sabotage.' Whatever happened, the fate of Wallace and Ewart was now sealed.

On the west bank of the Gironde, a few miles away from all this activity, Hasler and his three surviving men were trying to rest. While one kept watch, the others slept, but not for long as their peace was disturbed by the sound of a number of fishing boats passing close by as they emerged from the small river that ran up to the village of St Vivien. Several of the smaller boats then turned to port and beached themselves close by where the marines were hiding. At the same time a number of women appeared, walking along the shore towards the fishing boats, joining them on the beach and preparing breakfast on campfires.

It was not long before the villagers spotted the canoes and their occupants just a few yards away. Monsieur Yves Ardouin and his family, together with members of the Chaussat family, had come to the beach to work on the oyster beds bordering the river. The presence of the strange men with blackened faces would certainly have unnerved the civilians. Hasler decided to make himself known to them and ask for their cooperation.

The major asked his men to cover him with their weapons while he walked over and parleyed with the fishermen. He was met by Yves Ardouin. Hasler explained that he and his men were English soldiers and were their friends. He asked that no one be told of their presence. Ardouin was at first suspicious, fearing a German trap, but gradually realized that it was probably safest for him and his family to mind their own business and not to become involved.

Hasler returned to his hide and the fishermen to their meal. Both parties watched each other surreptitiously, not knowing whether or not the other would prove to be mendacious. The fishermen finished their food and began working on the oyster beds along with the women. When their work was done, they returned to their boats and slipped away on the incoming tide, but before they left Yves Ardouin came across to Hasler with a gift of bread. As the major thanked the Frenchman he was told that there was a group of Germans building some sort of military installation downstream nearby and that Hasler and his men should be on their guard.

Their wait that day was a long one, for the evening's flood tide was not due until 2330 hours. 'As this was low water springs it was necessary to man-handle the boats over nearly ¾ mile of sandy mud before we could launch them,' Hasler wrote later. 'The method employed was to drag the boats by their painters[2], fully loaded, which was only possible owing to the flat bottom and strong construction of the Cockle Mk II.'

Getting the boats clear of the outlying sand banks over which a ground swell was running in the form of small breaking waves was a precarious manoeuvre. The canoes had to be kept head-on into the foaming rollers while the men scrambled clear of the clinging mud and into the craft. Once out into the main stream, paddling with long deliberate strokes, they soon began to get their minds back on to their mission.

---

2 Short rope lines attached to each end of the canoe, used for mooring, towing, handling etc.

Picture of Yves Ardouin and his wife taken in the 1960s. Ardouin was the local fisherman who approached Hasler and his party with the offer of bread while the marines were sheltering in their hide at Pointe aux Oiseaux on the first day of the operation. (Royal Marines Museum Collection)

The regular movement of the dipping blades in and out of the icy water soon warmed them up. Although the night was pitch black, navigation was easy as the port-hand buoys marking the edge of the shipping channel showed a dim flashing blue light. The weather was calm without any cloud and visibility was good with a haze over both shores.

That night they switched their course over to the eastern side of the river, paddling through the night, keeping approximately a mile offshore. After each hour's labour the canoes would come together for a short rest. It was arduous work. Beneath their tunics the men sweated profusely, but on the outside their faces and hands were bitterly cold, covered in frozen spray, with splashes of salt water freezing on their cockpit covers. As daylight approached Hasler began looking for a site in which to lie up for the day. He succeeded in locating a perfect place at his first attempt, almost immediately opposite the famous wine-growing village of St Estéphe. The canoes were hauled ashore into the thick hedging, which gave them good cover. A small 'dixie' stove was used to make hot water for a mug of tea but food was limited to so-called 'compo' rations – waxed cartons containing a complete but unpalatable meal of biscuits, cheese, Spam, sweets, cigarettes, chewing gum and tea.

The day in the second hide was uneventful until the time came to move off at 1845 hours. Maj Hasler later explained what happened: 'In order to catch as much of the tide as possible, we started somewhat earlier than was prudent. We were soon seen silhouetted against the western sky as we launched the boats by a Frenchman from the nearby farm that came to investigate. We repeated our story of the day

**DECEMBER 10
1942**

**1845 hours
Hasler and his
men set off for
Bordeaux.**

before and he seemed quite convinced by it, and was rather upset when we declined to go up to his house for a drink.'

This night's progress up the river was complicated by the state of the tides. During the hours of darkness there were only three hours of flood tide at the beginning of the night. Then the tide changed against Hasler's party and they had to hide up during six hours of ebb tide. When the tide flow turned once more, there was more three more hours of the flood tide to help them upriver. Hasler had decided to make for an island in mid-river for his lying-up place, which from aerial photographs appeared to be uninhabited.

When they arrived later that evening, they found the island to be virtually impenetrable, for its mud banks were almost vertical and were topped by 4–5ft-high reeds. After many attempts and a considerable waste of time, at 2045 hours the two cockles were eventually dragged out of the water and hidden in the dense undergrowth. Most of the men then managed to catch some sleep before Hasler roused them again at 0200 hours to continue with the mission, although this was a little early for they had to wait over 40 minutes for the ebb to stop.

The river was now becoming much narrower with many more islands in mid-stream. The width of the available channel became increasingly restricted and the canoes were forced to progress closer to land. The sound of their paddles seemed to echo over the still water and the men became uncomfortably conscious of the noise of their passage, for many of these islands were inhabited. After two hours the marines entered a stretch of the river that forced them to pass between a long thin island called Île Verte and the western bank of the Gironde (confusingly, the island had two other names: it was called the Île du Nord in the centre and Île Cazeau at the southern end). The proximity of the island to the mainland forced the men to make themselves as inconspicuous as possible by using single paddles and keeping close to the shore of the island, which was covered in tall reeds. Four more hours of paddling on the surging tide brought the two canoes to the southern end of the island where they came ashore to lie up for the third day.

Their first attempt to land on the Île Cazeau put them close to a German flak installation, forcing them to try again. They were eventually compelled to take the last possible position right on the southern tip of the island just as it became light. There was little cover to be had and they spent the day in the middle of a marshy field among some tall grass with their boats covered in netting. It was not the best of locations, but it was all that was available. During the daylight hours that followed they were surrounded by a herd of cows and at one point a man with his dog came within 100 yards of their hide but did not discover them.

Hasler's original intention was to make the attack on the ships in Bordeaux that night, 10/11 December, but delays from the outset had put his timetable behind schedule. His team was now still some distance short of where they wanted to be. If they paddled their way upriver to the port and attacked that night as originally planned, they would not have enough hours of darkness to withdraw back down the river to a suitable position from which to start the escape across France. Hasler decided that he would have to move closer to Bordeaux and seek another hide closer to the port from which to launch the attack on the following night, 11/12 December.

**DECEMBER 10
1942**

**2100 hours
Mackinnon and
Conway are
rescued from
their damaged
cockle by
fishermen.**

There was, however, one major problem with this change in the timetable. Two of the original canoes might still be on the river closing on the objective. Sgt Wallace and Marine Ewart had been the first to disappear in *Coalfish* when they were swept away in the first tide race and it was possible that they might well have continued with the operation to attack on the night of 10/11 December. Hasler, of course, was not aware that they had already been picked up by the enemy. Lt Mackinnon and Marine

Conway in *Cuttlefish* could also still be making their way to Bordeaux with their orders to attack that night. Hasler's change of plan could backfire on him, for if either of the other two cockles pressed home their attack as originally planned, the river would be alive with the enemy scouring the area day and night to discover the raiders before they could make their escape.

Indeed, Mackinnon and Conway were still at large and quite close to Hasler and his party on the same long island. Since becoming separated they had piloted *Cuttlefish* upriver and were hiding on the island's eastern shore just a few miles north of the major and his party. When Hasler and his men left their hide that night at 1845 hours to make for a location closer to Bordeaux from which to launch the attack the following night, Mackinnon and Conway also set out from the Île Cazeau. The major took his party up the centre of the river for a few miles before switching towards the western bank and single paddles in order to proceed with more stealth, while Mackinnon steered his canoe down the eastern side of the island towards the confluence of the Dordogne and Garonne, the position at which the two rivers joined together to become the Gironde.

At around 2100 hours just off this point, Bec d'Ambes, Mackinnon's cockle ran against some underwater obstacle that tore a long gash in the canvas sides. The boat quickly began to take in water and started sinking. There was just enough time to grab the escape kit before the two men had to take to the icy water. As Conway struggled furiously to get out of the craft the pocket on his trouser leg became caught in the canoe. For a while the two marines became separated as they struggled to stay afloat in the darkness while remaining as quiet as possible. With considerable effort

**DECEMBER 11
1942**

**0030 hours
Wallace and Ewart
are executed by
firing squad.**

Château Magnol, once the Château Dehez, was the German Naval Headquarters Bordeaux during the war. It was to this headquarters that Sgt Wallace and Marine Ewart were brought for their final interrogation and execution. The château is situated just outside the village of Blanquefort, a few miles from the city. It now houses the headquarters of a wine company and is not accessible to the public.

Distances Covered by Canoes Each Night

Night	Nautical Miles
7/8 December	23
8/9 December	22
9/10 December	15
10/11 December	9
11/12 December	22
Total Distance Paddled By Canoe	91

they eventually made it back to the island. The next day, by some stroke of remarkably good fortune, they were taken off the island by French fishermen and deposited on the mainland.

In the meantime, oblivious to the drama that was being played out a few miles away by Mackinnon and Conway, Hasler continued up the river in weather that was perfect for his clandestine mission – cloudy sky with occasional rain and a light southerly breeze. By 2300 hours he and his party had almost reached Bordeaux. Just short of the main port they passed underneath a small jetty and began looking for a place to lie up for the remainder of the night. They soon found a small gap in the reeds and slipped the two canoes inside. With the tide beginning to ebb, the boats dried out and the men made themselves comfortable for the night. They had settled down in a well-concealed hide, invisible to passing waterborne traffic.

Across the river two large merchant vessels, the *Alabama* and the *Tannenfels*, were tied up along the quayside of the Bassens South area of the docks. Hasler and his men had at last come face to face with the first of the blockade busters.

Whilst Hasler and his men bedded down for the night opposite Bassens South, just three miles away to the west two of their comrades were having to pay the price for their bravery in volunteering for such a dangerous mission. Sgt Wallace and Marine Ewart had been brought to the Headquarters of the Naval Officer in Charge Bordeaux at the Château du Dehez (now the Château Magnol) in Blanquefort. They had spent an unhappy few days as prisoners of first the German Navy and then the SD at the German Interrogation Section in Bordeaux and were now finally back with the German navy. At 0030 hours on 11 December the two men were taken out of the château into the grounds at the rear and placed before a naval firing squad made up of one officer and 16 men. An officer of the SD watched as Wallace and Ewart were tied to posts and shot. He was later able to report that, as instructed, the saboteurs had been executed by direction of the Führer.

The half-light of dawn confirmed that Hasler had indeed found a perfect hide the night before. The tall reeds allowed the men to spend the day standing up, a luxury not experienced before during daylight hours, owing to the cramped nature of their previous hiding places. Securely hidden by the high undergrowth, they watched ships and small craft moving along the open river. Overcast skies and a slight rain aided their concealment. To their rear they could hear the everyday sound of the voices of people going about their business and of traffic moving along the road that ran parallel to the river. They also had the opportunity of studying the two targets marked down to be attacked that night, but for the most part of the day the men slept, each taking his turn to keep watch.

The Attack

Hasler now made his final plan of attack. *Catfish* was to proceed along the western bank to the docks and deal with ships tied up on the quay that ran along the river. *Crayfish* would cross over to the other bank of the river and go upstream searching for targets on the east side of Bordeaux. If no suitable enemy ships could be found, its crew were to come back to Bassens South and attack the two ships lying opposite. Once they had made their attack, both crews were to retire downstream as far as a possible on the ebb tide before daylight, scuttle their cockles and then make their escape.

During the afternoon, while it was still light, Hasler ordered his men to start the preparations for the attack. The first thing to be done was to rearrange the stowage of the boats so as to have all the escape equipment in two bags and everything they needed for the night's work readily to hand. Next was the fusing of the mines. Each limpet was armed by unscrewing the fuse caps and inserting a glass ampoule of acetone with a strength that would take nine hours to dissolve the washer that retained the firing pin, slightly longer than was normal due to the coldness of the water. The fuse would be initiated when the time came for the attack to begin. Finally the 6ft rod necessary to place the mines on the ships below the waterline was located on each limpet in turn to check that it engaged and disengaged correctly.

As the daylight faded, the weather moderated and the night became clear and cold. The river was calm and flat with excellent visibility – not the perfect conditions for a covert operation. During the early part of the evening there was a moon, but this was timed to set at 2132 hours. Hasler decided that it would be prudent to wait until 2110 hours before moving out. This was about 30 minutes later than he would have liked – he was mindful of the need to allow as much time as possible to make the escape downriver before daylight. At 2100 hours the major gave the order to start the time fuses. One by one the marines tightened down the thumbscrew on each fuse until there was a faint click as the glass ampoule inside broke and released its corrosive liquid. The limpets were now primed to explode at the appropriate time. There was no going back from here; the attack had begun.

Both canoes left the lying up place at 2115 hours. The men wished each other good luck and said their goodbyes, promising to meet up in Portsmouth in a couple of months' time. *Crayfish* moved out across the river to the far bank while *Catfish* continued upriver close inshore. In just over an hour Hasler's craft reached the built-up outskirts of Bordeaux. As it moved closer to the quays and warehouses along the river, Hasler could clearly see that no blackout was in force and the whole area was lit by a great number of lights. So bright was the surrounding area that he guided *Catfish* further out into the waterway and was forced to hold a line about 200 yards offshore. Soon the entrance to the inner basin showed up on his right, its access lit by bright floodlights. Hasler moved even further out into the river to give the brightly illuminated lock gates to the submarine pens a wide berth.

A few more minutes and then he could see his prey. A long line of ships, some with lights blazing, tied up along the wide curve of the Quay Carnot. Hasler scanned the ships, trying to decide what types they were. He knew that as he got closer to the vessels their great steel walls would rise high above him and their overall shapes would be lost to him. He could see that the first was a tanker and knew that this was not a good target. Tankers had too many watertight compartments and could not be sunk with just a few limpets. Beyond the tanker were several more promising targets: first a cargo liner; then another cargo ship, the *Portland*, with a tanker double-banked on the outside of it; then another freighter, the *Dresden*, and further along yet another vessel that looked to be a likely object for his mines, but which had a small warship, a *Speerbrecher*, moored alongside. There were more ships further along the quay, but Hasler knew that it was unlikely he would have enough time to get that far. The tide was nearing its ebb and would soon become difficult for any further movement upriver.

Hasler now brought *Catfish* close into the side of the river and paddled past the first ship. She was the tanker and he was after better things. The major and Cpl Sparks also slipped silently by the second vessel. She was a reasonable target and Hasler earmarked her to be attacked on the way back if he had any limpets left. Next came a definite blockade buster, the *Portland*, but the tanker moored on the outside of it made the attachment of mines amidships a difficult proposition. The next vessel was the perfect target: a blockade runner, the *Dresden*, lying alone next to the quay.

Once alongside, Hasler stowed his paddle and signalled to Sparks. The corporal brought out the magnetic holdfast and attached it to the ship's hull, grabbing on to

The Raid: Bordeaux and the routes of *Catfish* and *Crayfish*

10–11 December 1942

Sixty-nine gruelling miles of paddling lead the two surviving cockles, *Catfish* and *Crayfish*, to the area of quays at Bordeaux and the Bassens South. The final day is spent in their last hide preparing for the attack then, at 2115 hours on 11th December, Major Hasler, Corporal Sparks, Corporal Laver and Marine Mills set off in their frail craft to begin the attack on the German blockade busters.

▼ LOCATIONS

1 Last hide (2300 hours, 10 December–2115 hours, 11 December)

2 Lock entrance

3 U-boat pens

KEY

Route of *Crayfish*

Route of *Catfish*

German vessel

QUAY BASSENS SOUTH

EVENTS Ⓐ - Ⓙ

A 2115 hours, the crews of *Catfish* and *Crayfish* leave their hide and begin their attack.

B Corporal Laver and Marine Mills in *Crayfish* cross the river and move upstream in an attempt to find targets on the eastern side of the River Garonne.

C Major Hasler and Corporal Sparks in *Catfish* move up river close to the west bank heading for the enemy ships in Bordeaux.

D *Catfish* is moved into midstream to keep clear of the entrance to the u-boat pens.

E Laver and Mills in *Crayfish* find no suitable targets on the eastern bank and so turn downstream to attack the ships tied up along the Bassens South.

F Hasler takes *Catfish* along the line of enemy ships in Bordeaux identifying likely targets and then places mines on the cargo liner *Dresden*.

G The tide eventually begins to turn forcing Hasler to manoeuvre *Catfish* back downstream to attack the German *Speerbrecher*, the *Portland* and an unidentified tanker.

H Laver and Mills place eight mines on the two ships, the *Alabama* and the *Tannenfels*, moored at Bassens South and then escape down the Garonne.

I Hasler and Sparks complete their attack and move swiftly downstream keeping to the centre of the river.

J Both *Catfish* and *Crayfish* move down river independently making for Blaye where the cockles will be scuttled.

The limpet mines used to attack the ships in Bordeaux were located in position on the vessel's hull beneath the water line with the means of a placing rod. The placing rod shown here has been hinged flat to save space in the canoes. When opened out and secured it measures over 6ft in length. This example is on display at the Combined Military Services Museum at Maldon in Essex. (Courtesy of Richard Wooldridge, Combined Military Services Museum)

the handle to keep the canoe motionless on the slight drift of the tide. Hasler then assembled the hinged sections of the placing rod to their full extent and reached into the cockle. He gently withdrew the first limpet, which he fixed securely on to the placing rod. Then he lowered the mine into the water as far as the rod would allow and brought it smoothly towards the side of the ship. The pull of the six horseshoe magnets swung the limpet on to the steel plating and attached themselves with a muffled boom. A quick twist on the placing rod freed it from the mine. One limpet secured, seven more to go.

The process was repeated twice more on the vessel as the marines continued with the attack. Then on to the next ship. This one proved to be difficult. The German *Speerbrecher* on the outside of the freighter was ablaze with light, making it extremely risky to get behind without being seen. Hasler decided to attack the warship instead and planted two limpets near the inshore frigate's engine room. By this time the tide was on the turn and any further progress upstream was impractical; it was time to turn back.

Hasler and Sparks brought *Catfish* away from the side of the warship and began the intricate manoeuvre on the now ebbing tide to bring the bow of the craft around. Just then calamity struck. They heard heavy footsteps behind them on the deck of the *Speerbrecher* and a flashlight was turned on, catching them in its beam. A sentry on the warship had seen something in the water. The two marines quickly brought the cockle close into the enemy frigate and assumed the head-down, low position in the canoe. They remained motionless and let the tide carry them slowly along the ship's side. The sentry tried to keep the beam of his torch on the canoe as he followed it along the deck. The cockles' camouflage and the dark colours of the marines' clothing broke up the outline of the manned craft, no doubt confusing the German seaman. In the dark night it was easy to confuse the canoe for a floating log or other debris on the river. Hasler and Sparks drifted along with the tide, expecting that at any moment a shot would ring out and the alarm raised. Above them they could hear the heavy footsteps of the sentry as he kept pace with them on the deck above.

When the canoe reached the end of the ship Hasler eased the cockle under its bows and signalled to Sparks to silently clamp the holdfast on to the warship. They had slipped from view of the enemy sentry above them, although they could still hear his movements as he shifted position to search the surrounding water with his torch. After probing the darkness, the torch went out, but the sentry remained. For a while there was stalemate as neither party moved. Then, after several more minutes, Hasler motioned to Sparks to cast off and allow the cockle to drift slowly downstream on the tide.

Once again the two marines crouched low and immobile in their cockle to lessen their silhouette, praying that they would not be discovered. It was an agonizing few minutes for the two marines; unable to look round or move a single muscle they remained bent double until they were swallowed up by the darkness away from the view of the decks of the *Speerbrecher*.

They passed the vessel they had previously mined and came to the tanker with the freighter inboard of it. The cargo ship, the *Portland*, was Hasler's goal but the presence of the tanker prevented him from planting his mines amidships of the blockade buster. Instead he decided to use his limpets on the bows and the stern of the cargo ship. With a few dips of their paddles and the pull of the tide, *Catfish* was guided between the bows of the tanker and the freighter. Before the crew could get to work, however, the two ships began to swing towards each other on the swirling current of the ebb tide. Just in time, the marines were able to spread their arms and push their cockle backwards before being crushed by the towering steel walls closing about them.

The curve of the Quai des Chartrons at Bordeaux. This particular stretch of the harbour is the approximate location of the German *Speerbrecher* warship attacked by Hasler and Sparks during the raid. (Ken Ford)

A few frantic backstrokes with their paddles against the tidal flow brought them clear to safety. Hasler decided to try his luck at the stern of the ship.

This last mining attempt was completely successful. While Sparks kept the canoe stationary, Hasler planted two limpets on the stern of the *Portland* and then one on the tanker. All their work was now done: eight limpet mines placed on four separate ships. The major turned around to his corporal and with a beaming smile shook the marine's hand vigorously. Mission accomplished; all that was left now was to make their escape. Hasler brought his craft out into the darkness of mid-river and the two began paddling with renewed energy. With the tide running in their favour, and the canoes lightened by the shedding of their bomb load, the cockle was able to slice quickly through the water.

On the other side of the river the crew of *Crayfish* had also had a successful night. Cpl Laver and Marine Mills had paddled their way up the eastern side of the Garonne to the area opposite Bordeaux without finding any suitable targets and so came back to the two cargo ships tied up in Bassens South. Here they placed five limpets on the *Alabama* and three on the smaller cargo liner, the *Tannenfels*, before making their escape. No sign of the enemy had been seen during the attack.

The crews of both *Catfish* and *Crayfish* were now intent on making their escape with all speed. Both craft were being driven forward with long deliberate strokes so as to put as much distance as possible between themselves and the chaos that would soon be erupting in Bordeaux. Some ten miles downriver, close by the end of the Île Cazeau, Hasler and Sparks stopped to have a short rest in mid-stream. Much to their alarm they suddenly heard the sound of movement from behind getting closer and closer. Before they could react, a small craft came paddling towards them from out of the darkness. It was Laver and Mills in *Crayfish*. By sheer chance the two men had caught up with their commander while making their escape.

All four men were elated to see each other, especially Hasler, who was pleased to learn that Laver and Mills had made successful attacks on the ships at Bassens South and had placed all eight of their limpets on good targets. Laver asked if both cockles could continue downriver together for company and Hasler agreed. However, he stressed that on reaching the area of Blaye they must separate and make their escape independently. It was much too dangerous for four men to be seen travelling on the roads together.

The Escape

After a short rest the journey continued. But first, in order to make the most use of the low water slack, some caution was abandoned to speed up the move as Hasler later recorded: 'We proceeded in mid-stream using double paddles, and although we must have been clearly visible and audible from at least 200 yards away, we did not see any further signs of life.' By 0600 hours the flood tide had begun to turn. Fortunately by that time they had reached Blaye and had carried on for a mile past the village. At this point Laver and Mills separated from the group, with each of the men once again wishing the others good luck. Hasler and Sparks continued downstream for another quarter of a mile and came ashore close by the small hamlet of St Genés-de-Blaye.

It was now time for Hasler and Sparks to say goodbye to their cockle. The process was repeated by Laver and Mills a quarter of a mile or so away. The escape kits were removed from the craft before each small boat was slashed with a knife and pushed out into the Gironde to sink. The incoming tide swirled the doomed canoes a short distance away before they slipped slowly into the dark water. In a few moments they were gone. The four marines would now have to continue with their escape on foot. Their instructions were clear, as Hasler later recorded: 'When starting on the overland escape, get well clear of the river (say 10 miles), moving by night and in uniform. Then try to contact friendly farmers or peasants, borrow civilian clothes, hide uniforms and weapons and proceed by day.'

Also at large were Mackinnon and Conway, the crew of *Cuttlefish*. From captured German reports it appears that they had begun their escape overland a day earlier, after their canoe was damaged off the Bec d'Ambes. They were initially befriended by French civilians and made it as far as La Réole before eventually being arrested after betrayal to the Vichy Police by one of the locals. The two Royal Marines were immediately handed over to the Germans and returned to the SD at Bordeaux for interrogation.

Hasler and Sparks began their escape from the river bank two miles downriver from Blaye. All the raiders has been given maps of France and been told to make for the village of Ruffec, some 70 miles north-east of Bordeaux. Here members of the French Resistance had been warned to look out for them. Once contact had been made the escapees would be passed over to the 'Marie-Claire' network and moved down the escape chain through Vichy France to the Spanish border. The route would initially take them in the opposite direction to Spain, for the most obvious direct route out of France to the south-west was sure to be searched thoroughly by German and the Vichy French forces once the raid on Bordeaux had been detected.

On the first day the two men moved by night and rested up by day. They travelled to the north-east avoiding roads and villages, moving across fields and along cart tracks. Their most pressing need was to obtain civilian clothes so that they might blend in with the local population, but first they had to get as far away from the river as possible. On the morning of 13 December, the second day of the escape, Hasler decided to approach a farmhouse and ask for clothes. He was met with a reception that would be repeated again and again throughout the whole of the journey. The moment he opened his mouth a look of fear came over the faces of all he met. He explained that the two of them were English soldiers escaping the Germans and wanted help, a request that placed a great strain on the locals. To give such help the French people placed their lives and those of their families at risk from both the Germans and from the Vichy French police. They all knew that the punishment for helping the British was immediate arrest and confinement in a concentration camp or death.

At that first farmhouse Hasler and Sparks received a black beret and a cloth cap. The poor farmer could spare nothing else. Later that day two other houses were visited but with no success; the inhabitants could not close the door on the fugitive Englishmen fast enough. Finally at a remote farmhouse they got lucky, very lucky indeed. A woman answered their knock and listened to their request. She then told them to wait and disappeared back inside. Eventually she returned carrying two pairs of trousers and a jacket. Both were old and threadbare, but at least they were civilian clothes. The woman even provided them with a sack to carry their belongings. They could not thank her enough for this brave act.

Hasler and Sparks retired to a wood to effect a change in their status from Royal Marines to French peasants. Off came their uniform trousers and camouflaged anoraks with their badges of rank, to be replaced with rustic attire. Their weapons were discarded and buried along with their service clothing. Sparks wore the jacket, with Hasler having just his blue pullover to keep out the cold. Their gloves, thick socks and balaclavas they put into the sack. They could now pass for itinerant peasants of whom few people took notice.

Their journey continued with another two or three calls at isolated houses. They managed to beg a second sack and a rough coat to complete their outfits. With renewed confidence they no longer used byways and tracks, but ventured along the highways. They were not yet ready for the main roads, but kept progress to side roads that linked together smaller villages, none of whose inhabitants seemed to note their passing as being anything other than normal. It did mean that their route to Ruffec was not direct, but with the aid of their compass they could keep their heading roughly north-east.

As each day progressed the journey became harder. The rations they had brought were enough to last them only a few days and by the end of the third day on the road the supply was almost gone. The cold December weather was also taking its toll, for the intermittent rain that had plagued their march from the start had left them wet to the skin. Nights were still being spent in the open with little cover. On that day, 14 December, Cpl Laver and Marine Mills were picked up by the French police in the village of La Garde, just 12 miles away from Hasler and Sparks, and handed over to the Germans. Of the ten men who left HMS *Tuna* just seven days previously, now only the major and his corporal still remained at liberty.

With their food virtually gone and their physical condition deteriorating, the two marines realized that they would now have to ask for food and shelter each day from the locals. Not surprisingly this was difficult to find, but there were acts of kindness shown to them. During the day there was the gift of some bread and chicken and that

Escape route taken by
Hasler and Sparks.

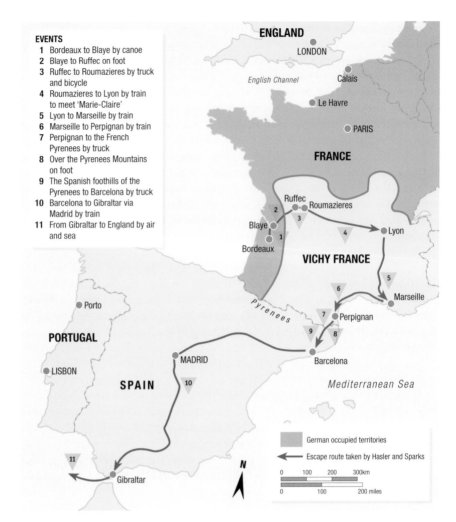

EVENTS
1 Bordeaux to Blaye by canoe
2 Blaye to Ruffec on foot
3 Ruffec to Roumazieres by truck
  and bicycle
4 Roumazieres to Lyon by train
  to meet 'Marie-Claire'
5 Lyon to Marseille by train
6 Marseille to Perpignan by train
7 Perpignan to the French
  Pyrenees by truck
8 Over the Pyrenees Mountains
  on foot
9 The Spanish foothills of the
  Pyrenees to Barcelona by truck
10 Barcelona to Gibraltar via
  Madrid by train
11 From Gibraltar to England by air
  and sea

DECEMBER 11 1942

2100 hours Hasler gives the order to start the time fuses and approach the docks.

DECEMBER 12 1942

Hasler and Sparks begin their escape on foot towards Spain.

night a more pleasant welcome from a Communist woodcutter. The man was at first very aggressive towards the fugitives, driven no doubt by fear, but once he had been convinced that they were indeed British soldiers the whole wealth of his sparse hospitality was offered to them. They were given a feast of a meal and a soft bed on which to rest. The man was a fierce patriot and the night was enlivened by the woodcutter's tirade of hatred aimed at the Germans. He pleaded with Hasler to have the RAF drop arms so that he might kill Germans. He also requested that the BBC broadcast a message to him when they got back to England showing that they were safe. The next morning there was time for a large breakfast and a complete wash and shave. A much refreshed Hasler and Sparks set out towards Ruffec that day with renewed vigour and with food in their sack.

As the escape continued the two men became more confident. The more people they saw the more they felt that they blended in. At the small town of St Même-les-Carrières they walked straight into a party of Germans who took not the slightest notice of them. To the Germans they looked just like any other Frenchman. During the day they ate the food given to them by the woodcutter and that night they found shelter in a hut by the side of a railway. According to their map they were 23 miles from Ruffec.

The next day they walked 15 miles through non-stop rain. Towards evening they knew that they would have to beg for food and perhaps find shelter. In the village of

Beaunac they had little success for they were turned away from house after house until just before dark. A friendly farmer finally gave them some bread and allowed them to sleep in his barn. Their rest did not last long, for the farmer soon roused them from their sleep and told them they must go. Some villagers, alarmed by their presence, had informed the police. In some haste they once more set off into the pouring rain towards their goal. Two hours along the road they found an isolated haystack and, after making a substantial hole in its base, they crawled inside and collapse into a deep sleep.

The next morning they awoke tired and hungry. It was just nine miles to Ruffec and Hasler was anxious to get there as quickly as possible. Once more they steeled themselves to tackle the driving rain. Spirits were low and both men were apprehensive about making a connection with the French Resistance. They had no place set aside for the rendezvous, nor did they have any names of whom to make contact with; they knew only that someone in the town would be looking out for them. All they could do was to plod on and hope that this day would bring some respite from their predicament and assistance from people with anti-German sentiments who were friendly to the British.

Hasler and Sparks approached Ruffec with some expectations of help. If they had known the true situation they might well have been even more concerned than they were, for the local Resistance had no idea that they were coming. The escape

**DECEMBER 12
1942**

**0700–1305 hours
13 explosions rip
into ships at
Bordeaux.**

**DECEMBER 14
1942**

**Cpl Laver and Marine
Mills picked up by
French police and
handed over to the
Germans.**

Bill Sparks (right) behind the plaque on the cottage at Napres where he and Maj Hasler sheltered during their trek from the River Gironde to Ruffec. The memorial acknowledges the help that the woodcutter and his family gave to the two fugitives and was unveiled in 2002. (Royal Marines Museum Collection)

In 2002 Bill Sparks once again sits in the woodcutter's cottage where he and Hasler spent a night during their escape. The tiny cottage of La Maison de Clodomir is one of the places commemorated on the 'Souvenir *Frankton*' walk from the River Gironde to Ruffec that was set up by the French to honour the men who took part in the raid. (Royal Marines Museum Collection)

organization that they had hoped to be in contact with in Ruffec was run by an Englishwoman, Mary Lindell. Unfortunately she was then in hospital after having been hit by a car. No radio message had got though to her about the imminent arrival of escapees from Operation *Frankton*.

Mary Lindell was a truly remarkable woman. She had served during World War I as a nurse with the British and later the French Red Cross, and had received decorations for gallantry from both the French and Russians. She later married a French nobleman, Count de Milleville. At the start of World War II Mary Lindell lived in Paris and, after the Nazi occupation of northern France, began organizing the escape of groups of vulnerable people across the borders into the unoccupied zone. She was caught, interrogated and imprisoned by the Gestapo but eventually managed to escape to England. There she was recruited by MI9 and returned to France where, with the aid of her two sons Maurice and Oky, set up an escape route for downed British airmen with contacts at the Hôtel de France in Ruffec. She had been given the codename 'Marie-Claire' and her organization became the Marie-Claire Line.

Maj Hasler and Cpl Sparks arrived in Ruffec during the morning of 18 December, at the end of their 100-mile trek from the banks of the River Gironde. The two men walked into the town and were soon confronted with the question of what to do next. They were wet through to the skin, extremely tired and very hungry. Of course, they did not expect a welcoming committee, but they were hoping that someone would quickly spot them for what they were – two out-of-place 'deadbeats' – and approach them. They walked down the main street from west to east, stopping to look intently and slowly in every shop window, at every notice board, at every friendly face and at everything of interest they could find. There was no contact from anybody, so they turned around and retraced their steps in the same manner from east to west; still nothing.

By this time hunger had got the better of the two men and Hasler agreed with Sparks that they should take the risk of entering a café for something to eat. They chose a small bistro, the Toque Blanche café; it looked as though it was frequented by working men, so their rough clothing might not be conspicuous. It was lunchtime and the café had a number of customers. Choosing a table in the corner away from the others the major ordered soup and wine from the proprietor, Madame Mandinaud. They ate their meal as slowly as possible, hoping that the other diners would leave so that Hasler could approach the owner without raising any interest from the customers. When they had finished the other people showed no signs of leaving. Hasler ordered more of the same for them both and they lingered once again for some time over their sparse meal. The two men gradually became conscious of the fact that they might soon be asked to leave and so Hasler called for the bill.

Madame Mandinaud did not write out a bill, but told Hasler directly of the amount. The major handed her a 500-franc note with a small pencilled message from him wrapped inside explaining they were British soldiers and needed help. When she got to the till she read the note and went back to ask the pair to remain at the table. After the café had emptied, Madame Mandinaud led them up to a guest room and asked them to stay there while she went for help. By sheer good fortune they had stumbled on someone who had sympathy with their cause. A short while later she returned with three men, one of whom was her brother René. The other two were Jean Mariaud, a principal organizer with the local Resistance, and Monsieur Paillet,

Mary Lindell, Comtesse de Milleville, organizer of the 'Marie Claire' escape route through France into Spain. She and her son helped to get Hasler and Sparks from the rendezvous with the French Resistance in Ruffec to her organization in Lyons for onward passage to Gibraltar. (Royal Marines Museum Collection)

a retired English teacher. At first the men were suspicious of the marines, fearing a German trap, but after some questioning the Frenchmen eventually believed Hasler's story and said they would help. Paillet had asked Sparks a question and his reply convinced him that Sparks was English: 'He is a Cockney', Paillet reportedly remarked. 'No German could replicate that accent.' The marines had at last made contact with the Resistance.

The next day Mariaud and his brother-in-law took the two marines in a baker's van to the farm of Armand Dubreuille, where they remained, waiting for contact with the now disjointed Marie-Claire escape network. Finally, after a long and tedious stay of three weeks, they were collected and absorbed into the organization. From here on they became parcels to be handed from contact to contact in a long and nerve-wracking round of clandestine movements across France. There were extended periods of waiting in a number of safe houses as the two Englishmen were handed on down the escape chain.

Details of the attack made by Maj Hasler and Cpl Sparks in *Catfish* on the ships along the quay at Bordeaux. This diagram was drawn by Maj Hasler and was included in his post-raid report, which is now housed at the National Archives in Kew, London. (Crown Copyright from the National Archives)

Contact was made with Marie-Claire's son Maurice in January. A few weeks later they were taken to Lyons to meet with Mary Lindell herself. Through the leader of the Marie-Claire network Hasler was able to get a coded message back to COHQ via Switzerland, outlining the success of their mission and giving as much information as possible on the fates of other members of the group. From Lyons the two men were taken by rail to Marseilles and then to Perpignan. After a short wait a truck arrived to take them to the foothills of the Pyrenees. Here they were handed over to two Basque mountaineers who became their guides for the arduous trek over the mountains into Spain and then on to Barcelona where they made contact with the British consulate. The British vice-consul then arranged for onward transmission to Gibraltar via Madrid. Once inside the safety of the British colony Hasler was returned to England with the highest priority for debriefing. Sparks was to follow later at a more leisurely pace by sea. By early April 1943, the last surviving Cockleshell Heroes were back in England.

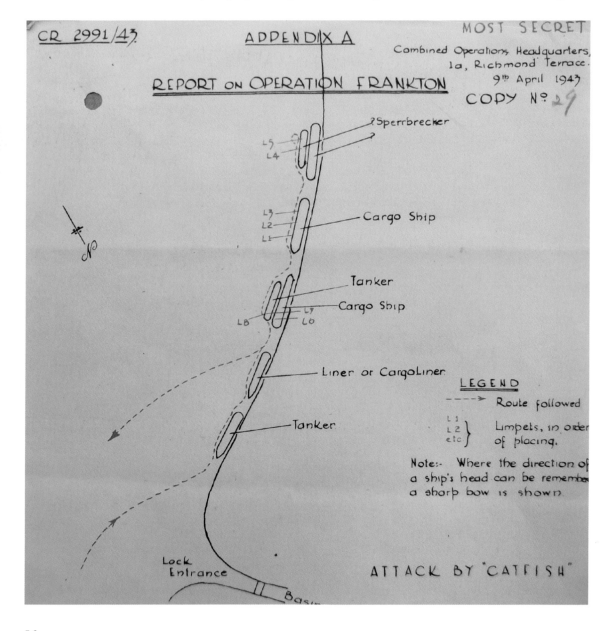

ANALYSIS

At 0700 hours on 12 December the still morning air along the quays at Bordeaux was shattered by an underwater explosion. Great plumes of water rose vertically from the side of hatch No. 5 on the *Alabama* tied up along Bassens South at Bordeaux. A hole measuring almost one and a half metres by one metre by German calculations had been blown on the ship's port side and water began to pour in. Three minutes later another explosion near hatch No. 1 appeared to be even larger than the first, for a splinter from the blast tore a hole in the ship's starboard side opposite. Damage parties immediately set to work trying to save the ship while the Germans tried to discover the cause of the explosions. Initial thoughts were that the damage was done by floating mines, most likely dropped by the RAF, but when a third explosion ripped into the ship at 0800 hours, it was clear that this was not the case.

At 0830 hours there was another underwater explosion, this time on the ship adjacent to the *Alabama*, the *Tannenfels*. This was soon followed by an explosion on the *Dresden*, upstream on the quayside at Bordeaux. Throughout the morning there were more explosions on the three ships and at 0955 hours the *Portland* was rocked by a blast. At 1030 hours, a fifth ship, the *Speerbrecher*, an inshore minelayer, was drenched with spray when an explosion occurred on its seaward side, although no damage was done to the vessel. This was most likely from a limpet mine that had dropped off the ship's side and exploded harmlessly on the river bed.

During that morning a total of 13 explosions took place along the river between 0700 hours and 1305 hours. It was clear to the German naval commander that the blasts were the work of a military raid that was most likely linked with the two British marines he had executed in the early hours of the previous morning at his headquarters

DECEMBER 18 1942

Hasler and Sparks arrive in Ruffec.

MARCH 1943

Hasler and Sparks cross the Pyrenees into Spain.

Post-war picture of Hasler and Sparks taken at the Château Magnol at Blanquefort outside Bordeaux. They are visiting the site of the execution of Sgt Wallace and Marine Ewart, an event that was commemorated by the plaque seen on the wall behind them. (Royal Marines Museum Collection)

in the Château du Dehez. How he must have rued the decision, made by an authority much higher than him, to have them shot in such haste, for with their deaths there was no further possibility of extracting more information about the attack.

A German report captured at the end of the war listed the damage done to the ships in Bordeaux. Water penetrated the *Alabama* through hatches 4 and 5. The same was true for *Tannenfels* through hatches 2 and 3, which created a list of 24 degrees. Countermeasures were undertaken to successfully prevent the ship from capsizing. In the *Dresden*, holds 4, 5, 6 and 7 filled with water and the stern of the ship sank to the bottom. Leaks were sealed by 2330 hours but it took until 14 December for the holds to be emptied. Little water penetrated the *Portland* and the hole was soon provisionally sealed. All the ships were empty at the time of the explosions. Further work was undertaken by divers and it was possible to seal the *Dresden* and the *Tannenfels* while they were partially in a sinking condition. The repairs allowed them to be floated at the next high tide and they remained afloat. The overall assessment was that the damage was reported to be slight.

Over the next few days the realization of just how far the defences along the Gironde and Garonne had been penetrated became clear. British forces had managed to move 60 miles up the river through a number of German positions to strike at a fully manned seaport without interception. There was also concern that the raiders were still at large, as the size of the British commando group was not known. Even more galling to the Germans was the fact that saboteurs had been captured days before the attack but this had not resulted in raised security levels in the port.

New security measures were immediately devised to try to intercept the fleeing raiders and to prevent any further such attacks. The new measures were far-reaching and tied up a huge amount of manpower. The most important of these were as follows: ships in the harbour were to be illuminated from shore as from 12 December; patrols and pickets guarding shore installations were to be strengthened and patrols in the harbour area increased; a boat was to patrol the whole of the harbour, including the Bassens, at night; and the Pauillac floating dock, the gate of the Gironde wharf and the stone bridge at Bordeaux were to be protected by river booms. At the river estuary, the area was to be swept by searchlights and fired on when any unknown radar contact was made. Later even more security measures were taken, including placing two sentries on each merchant ship and, if an explosion occurred on the side of a ship, the sides of all ships in the vicinity were to be searched with poles to detect any further charges. The Gironde estuary was to be guarded by two further patrol vessels, three searchlight batteries and by land patrols on either side of the river.

Back in England little news of the raid had been received. There had been an official announcement made by German High Command just after Wallace and Ewart were captured during the first night, which stated: 'On 8 December a small British sabotage squad was engaged at the mouth of the Gironde River and finished off in combat.' This news of course lowered spirits at COHQ and at Southsea and it looked for a while that the operation had been a failure. Nothing further was known until the brief message from Hasler via Marie-Claire's network was received in February.

It was not until the end of the war that a proper assessment could be made from captured documents of the damage inflicted on the ships in Bordeaux. The work of the blockade busters was certainly interfered with because of the raid, but it was the changing fortunes of the Allies in naval warfare and their growing strength in the oceans of the world that finally eliminated the seaborne trade between the Axis nations. From the end of 1942 a greater number of British, French and American warships patrolled the seaways off Africa looking for the blockade runners. The *Portland*, which had been damaged in the raid and later repaired and put to sea again in April 1943, was eventually intercepted off the coast of Dakar by the Free French cruiser *George Leygues* and scuttled by her crew before capture. During 1943 only one blockade runner actually made it from Japan back to France and that voyage ended in disaster. The *Osorno* sailing from Kobe was damaged at the mouth of the River Gironde on 2 October but beached in such a position that her cargo was saved. All other passages by surface ships between Japan and France were intercepted and sunk. By 1944 all the blockade busters had been dealt with, but some small trade with the Far East was still being carried out using large German and Japanese submarines.

Two days after the mines had exploded in Bordeaux, Laver and Mills were captured by French police and brought to the police prison in the city. Here they were handed over to the German SD. By now the Germans had a very good idea of what the marines had been up to and were determined to find out more about the raid and its organization. Hitler's 'immediately kill commandos' directive seems to have been ignored in the case of Laver and Mills, for they remained in custody and under

On 26 November 1976, Cpl Bill Sparks re-enacts the first part of his voyage during Operation *Frankton* in a modern canoe launched from the submarine HMS *Narwhal*. (Royal Marines Museum Collection)

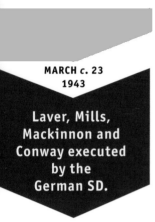

MARCH c. 23 1943

Laver, Mills, Mackinnon and Conway executed by the German SD.

interrogation in Bordeaux for some time, as did Mackinnon and Conway following their capture. Certainly the interrogation was severe, perhaps even made under torture, for it is clear from post-war documents that the Germans discovered almost all they wanted to know about the raid, including the training they received, how they got to France and the composition of their group.

The four Royal Marines were first questioned at Bordeaux until, in early January 1943, they were removed to Dulag Nord at Wilhelmshaven in Germany. Here they were interrogated at length by the German Naval Intelligence Section. Some time later they appear to have been taken to Paris and handed over to the Gestapo. After more questioning and most likely more torture it eventually became clear to their captors that there was little more to be learned from the prisoners. The German SD were now done with them and they were summarily executed some time around 23 March 1943. German accounts indicate that they were all buried in Bagneux Cemetery, Paris, although no local records confirm this, nor is there any positive evidence of the location of their burials.

After the war the Judge Advocate General's (JAG) Office investigated all the shootings as war crimes. The executions were carried out under Hitler's 'shoot commandos' order and it was therefore difficult to place ultimate responsibility with any individual officer. However, JAG investigators felt they had a prima facie case against Admiral Bachmann, for he had personally ordered the execution of Wallace and Ewart. The Führer's order had directed that any saboteurs were to be handed over to the SD for immediate execution. In ordering the initial interrogation to be carried out by German naval staff, personally instructing that the two marines be shot immediately afterwards and having naval personnel carry out the shooting, Bachmann had instigated the actions under his authority and had therefore been guilty of a war crime. An 'all stations' search was made for Admiral Bachmann at the end of the war, which even included visiting his wife at her home. No sign of the admiral was ever found and it was later established that he had been killed towards the end of the conflict on 2 April 1945 while serving in the Willebadessen district of Warburg in Germany.

When Hasler arrived back in England he was able to give a full account of the raid and helped to interpret the lessons that could be learned from the operation. Both he and Cpl Sparks resumed their service career almost immediately. Maj Hasler returned to Southsea to continue his command of the RMBPD and to use his inventive mind to design canoes for further covert operations. He developed the motorized submersible canoe and did pioneering work on underwater swimming. His efforts helped the development of two other organizations, the Combined Operations Pilotage Parties (COPPs), which landed men on occupied enemy beaches to carry out undercover reconnaissance, and the Sea Reconnaissance Unit (SRU), which used underwater swimmers to enter enemy-controlled harbours. The exploding motor boat that gave rise to the formation of the RMBPD never saw action during the conflict. After the war LtCol Hasler became a noted yachtsman and journalist involved in all aspects of recreational sailing. He died in 1987. Cpl Sparks later served with the Royal Marines in Burma, Africa and Italy and left the army in 1946 to become a trolley-bus driver. He remained with London Transport until his retirement, although he did spend a year in Malaya as a policeman during the Emergency in 1952. Bill Sparks died in 2002.

Maj 'Blondie' Hasler and Cpl Bill Sparks were both given awards for their part in the successful outcome of Operation *Frankton*. Hasler received the Distinguished Service Order (DSO) and Sparks the Distinguished Service Medal (DSM). Cpl Laver and Marine Mills were Mentioned in Dispatches, for there is no posthumous award of the DSM.

APRIL 1943

Sparks arrives back in England by sea.

CONCLUSION

The raid on Bordeaux harbour by Maj Hasler's Royal Marine Boom Patrol Detachment was one of the most remarkable of the war. While the raid only disrupted the blockade busters, rather than stopping them altogether, it struck at the heart of Germany's war effort and its security. It showed, as did many other raids on German-occupied territory, that no German, nor any German property or installation, was safe from attack. A party of just 12 men had set out to wreak havoc on German blockade busters, and wreak havoc they did, succeeding where the RAF could not, and providing a huge morale boost for the beleaguered British population.

The raid had repercussions far beyond the environs of Bordeaux, and the despicable acts meted out to those of the group who were captured ensured that the event will never be forgotten. The operation was unusual as an act of war, for none of the raiders ever came face to face with the enemy until they were caught. Nor was there any shot fired, grenade thrown or individual German killed during the whole operation. And yet the Cockleshell Raid is the stuff of legend, seen, quite rightly, as a magnificent military success. Six of the original 12 were killed by the Germans, two did not take part, two were drowned and the remaining two returned as heroes. When compared to the great loss of life endured during even relatively small operations elsewhere in the war, the death toll was light. Nonetheless, the manner of the deaths – execution even though they were legitimate soldiers in uniform – marks the operation out to be a human tragedy that has captured the public's imagination.

In 1955 a full-length feature film was made by Warwick Films called *The Cockleshell Heroes*. Hasler and Sparks were employed as advisers and the film purported to be an account of the raid. Certainly some elements of the film were true, but, as with all war films, those few elements of truth were surrounded with much fiction to form an 'entertainment'. *The Cockleshell Heroes* as an entertainment was first class; a British war film with a host of excellent actors. As history, it leaves much to be explained and much to be put right.

THE COCKLESHELL HEROES

This plaque, provided by Portsmouth City Council, was unveiled by Marine Bill Sparks DSM on 6th July 1992, In the presence of the Lord Mayor of Portsmouth, Councillor Jim Patey and the Chairman of the Leisure Committee Councillor Syd Rapson BEM, to mark the 50th Anniversary of this site which was used as a training base for the Royal Marine Boom Patrol Detachment, formed on 6th July 1942. This secret unit trained on the Solent for raids by canoe (Cockles) on Europe.

The most famous raid was made on German shipping in Bordeaux docks on 11th December 1942 by ten members of RMBPD, only two of these Cockleshell Heroes returned:

MAJ H HASLER, OBE DSO RM	LT J MACKINNON, RM
MNE W SPARKS, DSM	MNE J CONWAY
CPL A LAVER	SGT S WALLACE
MNE W MILLS	MNE R EWART
CPL G SHEARD	MNE D MOFFAT

This plaque reminds visitors that the area around Lumps Fort at Southsea was used as a training ground by the Royal Marine Boom Patrol Detachment during the war and it was from this site that the party of Royal Marines set out on Operation *Frankton*. (Ken Ford)

The two survivors of the raid on Bordeaux, Operation *Frankton*. Maj H. G. 'Blondie' Hasler (left) and Cpl Bill Sparks, shown together in at the unveiling of the memorial in Bordeaux that marks the site of the attack on the German ships in December 1942. (Royal Marines Museum Collection)

Following on from the film in 1956, the military historian C.E. Lucas Phillips produced a book also called *Cockleshell Heroes*. The author had access to many unreleased official documents to help put together his story. The book was written with the cooperation of the then LtCol 'Blondie' Hasler and the result was a comprehensive account of the RMBPD and of Operation *Frankton*. This was history put right.

In more recent times several documentaries have been made on Operation *Frankton* for television and the raid is once again back in the public eye. In France it has not been forgotten, for several monuments to the raid and to those who lost their lives or were executed have been dedicated. In England too there are monuments and memorials. One of the most interesting of remembrances is the formation of the 'Frankton Walk' in France, a tourist route that follows the journey taken by Hasler and Sparks between the River Gironde and Ruffec. It seems that the Cockleshell Raid will not be forgotten for many more years to come.

BIBLIOGRAPHY

There has, to my knowledge, been only one full account of Operation *Frankton* published, *Cockleshell Heroes* by C.E. Lucas Phillips. The two survivors of the raid, Hasler and Sparks, have both had biographies produced that covered the parts they played in the raid. When Lucas Phillips was writing his book back in the 1950s, the author was given exclusive access to the secret official files associated with the operation. In 1972 these documents were released to the public under the 30-year rule. They are now accessible to all in the National Archives at Kew in London. I have used these files extensively in this present account of Operation *Frankton* and have listed them and their contents below.

ADM 173   Log of HMS *Tuna*
ADM 202/310   War Diary of RMBPD
ADM 1/18344   Shooting of the captured marines and war crimes investigations
ADM 202/399   Maj Hasler's after-action report
DEF 2/216   Intelligence Reports prior to raid
DEF 2/217   Awards for those participating in the planning and execution of
               the raid

Further Reading

Lucas Phillips, C. E., *Cockleshell Heroes*, Heinemann, London, 1956

Southby-Tailyour, Ewen, *Blondie*, Leo Cooper, Barnsley, 1998

Sparks, William & Munn, Michael, *The Last of the Cockleshell Heroes*, Leo
   Cooper, London, 1992

Sparks, Bill, *Cockleshell Commando*, Leo Cooper, Barnsley, 2002

And, forthcoming as of the writing of this work:

Rees, Quentin, *Cockleshell Canoes*, Amberley Publishing, Stroud, 2009

INDEX

Figures in **bold** refer to illustrations